Hope for Parents of Troubled Teens

"*Hope for Parents of Troubled Teens* is an important book for all parents. Whether a child is rebellious, out of control, or just going through the growing pains of adolescence, Connie has valuable advice and a refreshing viewpoint. Hers is a message of hope for parents in pain. It is not just a how-to book, it is a shared journey of one who has been there."

—Dr. Jerry Cook
Author, conference speaker

Hope for Parents of Troubled Teens

A Practical Guide to Getting Them Back on Track

CONNIE RAE, LMHC

BETHANY HOUSE PUBLISHERS
a division of Baker Publishing Group
Minneapolis, Minnesota

Published by Bethany House Publishers
11400 Hampshire Avenue South
Bloomington, Minnesota 55438
www.bethanyhouse.com

Bethany House Publishers is a division of
Baker Publishing Group, Grand Rapids, Michigan

Printed in the United States of America

Library of Congress Cataloging-in-Publication Data
Rae, Connie.
Hope for parents of troubled teens : a practical guide to getting them back on track / Connie Rae.
p. cm.
Includes bibliographical references and index.
Summary: "A Christian counselor who went through very difficult years with her own teenage son gives parents hope and advice in dealing with troubled teenagers"—Provided by publisher.
ISBN 978–0–7642–0946–8 (pbk. : alk. paper)
1. Parenting—Religious aspects—Christianity. 2. Parenting. 3. Parent and teenager. I. Title.
BV4529.R33 2012
248.8'45—dc23 2011036844

Cover design by Greg Jackson, Thinkpen Design, Inc.

12 13 14 15 16 17 18 7 6 5 4 3 2 1

In keeping with biblical principles of creation stewardship, Baker Publishing Group advocates the responsible use of our natural resources. As a member of the Green Press Initiative, our company uses recycled paper when possible. The text paper of this book is composed in part of post-consumer waste.

Author's Note

It will be noted by the reader that many of the references to children and youth are in the male gender. This is because my own experiences were with a son. But there are also many chapters where male and female genders have been alternated. This has been done to avoid the awkwardness of the phrases "he or she" and "his or her." Please substitute the appropriate gender for your family situation as you read.

Contents

Acknowledgments

This book could not have been written without the experiences our family had with our own rebellious teenager. Thank you, son, for teaching us how to love—and to grow.

Thanks also to my husband, who experienced everything with me, and was a rock when I needed him. Thanks to our other children, who lived with their own challenges and were loyal to their brother in spite of it all.

To the many friends and "counselors" who prayed with us and for us during the turbulent times and were supportive in the original writing of this book many years ago—thanks.

To the hundreds of teenagers and parents I have had the privilege of counseling and walking with through your tough times—thank you for trusting me with your family's troubles.

And much appreciation and thanks to Andy McGuire, my editor at Bethany House, who believed in the message of the book and gave this first-time author the opportunity to become part of the Bethany House family.

Most important, there are no words to express my deepest reverence and praise to my Father, whose love and discipline made the difference—a simple thank-you is insufficient, but they are the only words I have. Thank you, Jesus, for all you've done.

Introduction

What Can You Do?

Adolescence can be an exciting time of growth and newness for parents and children. Many families make it through with relatively few battle scars and with an established sense of healthy interdependence. However, some young people get caught up in rebellious behavior that escalates into something serious.

This book has been written to bring hope and healing to families, especially to parents who are teetering on the edge of despair with their teenage children. I've been there. I've felt the pain and the hopelessness.

My family has experienced the message of this book. Our own rebellious child finally made it, but not until six long, hard years had passed. In the end, really the *beginning* for our son, it was God who brought about the miracle of change in his life. It was God who gave him the determination and strength to make decisions about his future. It was God who gave him the daily power to carry those decisions through. Mom and Dad, meanwhile, examined, evaluated, and reevaluated everything. It was a time of "growing and becoming," in spite of daily frightening circumstances, or maybe because of them.

When we were experiencing the worst with our teenage son, we wanted to know that somebody, *anybody,* understood what was happening to us. We heard a lot of comments like, "Oh, we're so sorry" or "There's nothing you can do. You just have to wait until he comes to his senses" or "Kick him out. Let him see what it feels like to be on his own" or "Make stronger rules; ground him." Though well-meaning, none of this was helpful.

There are no words, initially, to lift the heavy weight in your heart or to miraculously turn your child around to "see the light." What I often tell parents I work with is: "It's likely to get worse before it gets better." Not exactly what they want to hear. But it's the truth. And in the meantime, there are things we can, and should, do.

First, try to take the focus off thoughts like, *How could he/she do this to me?* and start thinking, *How can I help this child find his/her way?* This change in attitude goes a long way toward helping your own "bleeding" to stop.

Second, try to establish some kind of relationship with the warring teen. It's difficult, but do whatever you can to make this happen. They may ignore you or refuse your gestures, but try.

From there, please take the time to read this book and follow the suggestions for moving your family toward wholeness. There are no magic solutions. But I believe as you explore the "Something to Do" suggestions at the end of each chapter, there will be movement in the right direction. You are suffering. Your child is suffering in a different way. Do *something.*

The Bible tells us that *faith* without *works* is dead. The message of this book is that having *hope, faith,* and *trust,* means there are things we can *do* to make a difference in our relationship with our child, even if he does not respond to us as we would like him to.

But when the last authority figure has been talked with, when the final desperate measure has been taken, when the last shred of human wisdom has been tapped, hope may be all that is left. The

Scriptures tell us that *faith* is the substance of things *hoped* for, the evidence of things not seen. Hope rests in our faith in God, and our willingness to trust that He will do what we cannot do.

In addition to offering counsel to parents already in crisis, I would hope that some parents will read this book *before* their child's behavior becomes troublesome so they might avoid the upheaval and chaos that happens when a child loses his way. If you are a parent just entering the world of teenagers, and you haven't experienced any significant troubles yet, this book might help you circumvent problems that may lie ahead.

My earnest prayer is that you will find information, wisdom, and encouragement within these pages. I trust your family will be made whole.

Where Did This Kid Come From, Anyway? 1

We were driving to church—just my husband and I. Silently. Finally, I said, "Have we been too hard? Too strict? Too unbending? Maybe we should have given in more, let him do some things even if we weren't comfortable with them."

More silence. Then my husband replied, "He did everything he wanted to do—whether we OK'd it or not. Look where it got him. What else could we have done? What could we have done differently and still been true to our convictions?"

More silence. We were both thinking. Wondering. Steve was safe for the moment—in the county jail. It was amazing how the worries lifted when we knew where he was and that he couldn't get into more trouble—for the time being. He was remorseful. Again.

This was the third, or was it the fourth time he was incarcerated? The first times had been to juvenile detention. We celebrated his eighteenth birthday in a tiny room in juvenile hall—and then they moved him across the street to the county jail.

We were the ones responsible for his first arrest. After several incidents, promises made and broken, we went to the juvenile authorities and asked them to help us. They did. They arrested him and confined him. He was angry. The minute he got out, on probation with all kinds of restrictions, he was off to be with his friends—the same ones he was getting into trouble with. Then it was only a matter of time before he was picked up again—for possession of marijuana.

Steve had written checks on our family's meager bank account. He'd pawned family items. He'd "borrowed" his father's truck to run around in when he was supposed to be in school. He didn't have a license. His father taught in the junior high school across the street from the high school. Many times he left at the end of the day thinking he had parked his truck in one place and found it in another. Shaking his head, he blew it off to poor memory.

Then there was the day when he pulled into a neighborhood gas station to fill up the tank. "Man, your truck must really burn up the gas. Your son was just in here and filled it."

We had prayed that he would not get away with anything—and God honored our prayer. At one point we sat in the office of the probation officer (PO) with our son, hoping to find a way to stop this rush to destruction. He was in big trouble now. The PO was giving him the opportunity to confess to everything he had ever done, for immunity. Our son looked at us and with a solemn shake of his head, said, "They know *everything* I have ever done"; and then to us, "Have I missed anything?" We didn't think so. God was faithful, and we made sure our son and the probation officer knew it.

Out of jail once again, we helped him get a job. We let him be home again, as he earnestly attempted to get his life on track. But the temptations were too great, the will too weak, and he was back in trouble again.

Thanksgiving Eve, middle of the night, we received a phone call from the sheriff's office. He had been arrested, once again, for possession of marijuana. We were expecting a houseful of family and friends for Thanksgiving dinner. We were heartbroken, embarrassed, frightened, and we still had to "entertain."

It was hard to tell the family again. Everyone had hoped and prayed he was finally on the way to getting it together. We feared differently, but still we hoped. Still we prayed, "Whatever it takes."

So here we were.

The last time we had been in court with our son, the judge had said he didn't ever want to see him again before his desk. He made it clear that if there *was* a next time, he would go away for a long time.

Our son had had a three-year history of forging checks, auto theft, running away—all crimes within the family. We could have overlooked them. We could have excused them. We could have threatened and required restitution. In fact, we did all of those things. Nothing made a difference. We went to the authorities for backup, to force him into compliance—and now he was facing real prison time. We were fearful. We were remorseful. We wondered if our "righteousness" had condemned our son to imprisonment with felons, murderers, and rapists. What had we done?

Hope Becomes Reality

Today, Steve has been married more than twenty-five years and is the father of two grown children. He has been a successful businessman, an entrepreneur, a planner, and a developer. He is a good man. He honors his father and his mother and appreciates his siblings and extended family. Life has not always been easy. He learned his first trade while in a nine-month drug treatment program—the alternative to prison time. We hired a lawyer who very directly put it to Steve: prison or treatment program. You choose. He chose the treatment program with no hope that it would make a difference for him.

We were so fearful he would bolt again that we picked him up at the county jailhouse door, locked him in the backseat of the car (child locks!), held onto him from both sides while we stopped at the local music store to buy him a guitar (Christmas present), and three hours later, delivered him into the hands of the intake person at the treatment center. He knew he was free to leave at any time, but the moment he would do so, an all-points bulletin would be issued for his arrest, and his next stop would be prison. He stayed.

Two weeks after entering the program, they allowed him to call home—*our* Christmas present. "Mom, Dad, I want you to know I've turned my life over to Christ. I'm going to make it. I'll stay here as long as it takes." It took nine months.

Our Children Are Unique

Sometimes life seems so unfair. Just about the time we feel we are "getting it all together," along comes a precious little bundle of joy and energy who doesn't necessarily live up to our expectations. If we already have a child who is totally delightful (yes, they do exist!), the shock may be doubly staggering. And then we compare ourselves to that "perfect" family who has only happy, manageable children—or at least appears to. And we wonder.

It would be wonderful if all newborns were indeed a *tabula rasa,* as John Locke suggested back in the 1600s—a blank sheet of paper, upon which experience writes. We could be perfect parents, imprinting only the best things on our children's absorbent little minds, and they would all turn out wonderfully well. Or would they? What a burden to put upon the parents of the world!

No, God had a different plan. Each of our children is born with a unique and many-faceted personality. Dr. James Dobson of Focus on the Family said it this way: "Just as surely as some children are naturally compliant, there are others who seem to be defiant upon exit from the womb. They come into the world smoking a cigar and yelling about the temperature in the delivery room and the incompetence of the nursing staff. They expect meals to be served the instant they are ordered, and they demand every moment of mother's time."[1]

Most parents of more than one child are well aware of their children's temperament differences—especially the differences that are annoying or that cause family disturbances. But sometimes, in the dailiness of living, we lose sight of the individuality of the

1. James Dobson, *The New Strong-Willed Child* (Wheaton, IL: Tyndale House, 1972).

child. We find ourselves fighting with behaviors that might represent some special character trait that needs to be recognized and developed into a strength. In the immature expression of that trait, we find ourselves irritated and frustrated, so instead of analyzing the temperament of the child, we begin to kill something that might be quite important in years to come.

Dr. Roger Williams commented in his book *You Are Extraordinary* on a study that was done by the Menninger Foundation.[2] One hundred twenty-eight babies were observed from one month of age until almost eight months of age. Everything about them was watched carefully, from diaper habits to feeding, sleeping, playing, crying, bathing. Marked personality differences showed up as soon as they could be observed. Some babies were bold. Others were shy. Some reacted quickly to stimuli. Others didn't even seem to notice. Some could tolerate tension and frustration. Others fell apart. These were all babies considered "normal" in every sense of the word.

This distinctiveness, this uniqueness of the individual stays with each of our children as they mature. In spite of the fact that we make bold attempts to mold them into a particular pattern of our choice and convenience, they remain "who they are." Maybe if we could recognize "who they are" when they are small, we might avoid certain problems when they are bigger.

Training Our Children, for Better or Worse

Many parents quote Proverbs 22:6 to assure themselves that if they teach their children Christian ways, they will eventually come back to their early training. But this Scripture can also be taken as a warning: "Train up a child in the way he should go [and in keeping with his individual gift or bent], and when he is old he will not depart from it." This implies that if we are careful to discover the uniqueness that lies within our child and use that individuality

2. Roger Williams, *You Are Extraordinary* (New York: Pyramid Publications, 1976).

as a tool in our parenting, we will make a considerable positive impact on our child's life.

On the other hand, we can train our children *negatively* as well. If we neglect to train carefully, considering the individual needs of a particular youngster, we will unintentionally train them to go the wrong way. The impact of this kind of training may reach us when our children reach adolescence.

Psalm 139:13–18 describes the beauty of our individuality before God. The psalmist praises God for the fearful and awesome wonder of his birth. He speaks of being "intricately and curiously wrought [as if embroidered with various colors]" (v. 15). He marvels at the revelation that God's eyes saw his "unformed substance, and in Your book all the days [of my life] were written before ever they took shape, when as yet there was none of them" (v. 16). He wonders at the innumerable thoughts of God toward him, and revels in the knowledge that God loves him.

In the wisdom of God, each of our children has been born with a special capacity to love and serve God, and has been given the uniqueness of temperament to do the job well.

As parents, we often despair at the willfulness, the cockiness, the deceitfulness, the rebellious-type spirit we have seen in certain of our children. But maybe we have misinterpreted and mishandled an independent, creative, potential leader by our lack of understanding.

Another question parents often ask is how these kids can be so different when we've raised them basically the same way. Given the extraordinary differences we find in children, it is no wonder they do not, cannot, respond to similar circumstances in similar ways. Each brings his own distinctive interpretation to life situations and to his own unique needs. How each child perceives his wants being met will have a major effect on his understanding of his life.

Individualized Spaces

In addition to inborn personality traits, each child has certain specific adjustments to make as a direct result of his particular situation. Birth order in the family, genders of siblings, the number of children in the family, the multiple complexities of relationships between parents and children—all give each child a very individualized space within the family unit.

Also, parents change. Family structures change. Environments change. Sometimes families change drastically in cases of separation, divorce, or death. All of these have a direct influence on each of the children in our home—but the message of that influence may be different for each child.

Stages of Child Growth and Development

Just as each of our children is different from the others, so he is, paradoxically, very much the same in his stages of growing up. A quick course in Child Growth and Development might look something like this:[3]

BABIES	. . . Beautiful	. . . Bawling
ONES	. . . Winsome	. . . Warring
TWOS	. . . Tender	. . . Terrible
THREES	. . . Trusting	. . . Trying
FOURS	. . . Fun	. . . Fearful
FIVES	. . . Fabulous	. . . Fighting
SIX	. . . Sensitive	. . . Slugging
SEVEN	. . . Serious	. . . Sour
EIGHT	. . . Active	. . . Aching
NINE	. . . Nice	. . . Naughty
TEN	. . . Terrific	. . . Tempestuous
ELEVEN	. . . Evolving	. . . Escaping
TWELVE	. . . Tantalizing	. . . Troubled
TEENS	. . . Terrific	. . . TERRIFYING!

Some children seem to always be on the "good" side of the diagram, with maybe an occasional slip over to the "not-so-good."

3. Chart adapted from Frances L. Ilg and Louise Bates Ames, *The Gesell Institute's Child Behavior: From Birth to Ten* (New York: Harper & Row, 1955).

Others never seem to leave the "far right," and their parents are always coping with behavior that leaves them exhausted both mentally and physically, but especially emotionally. Still other children move back and forth between "easy-to-live-with" and "hard-to-live-with" relatively smoothly.

Each of these one-word descriptions is an overgeneralization, but it represents realistic and normal behavior for these general age categories. Within these categories, children respond to life and to circumstances depending upon their individual temperament, their own particular pattern of growth and general development—and even the time of day!

Parenting Styles

An equally important factor that influences our children's decisions and attitudes is the philosophy of child-rearing that each parent, individually, brings to the family. Most parents train their children in a way that seems comfortable to them. In the midst of much confusing and even contradicting "advice" from the experts (and not-so-expert), most mothers and fathers still develop their own way of dealing with their children. They may completely accept the way they were raised and follow through with their own children. Or they may completely reject their parents' practices, or fall somewhere in between. Whatever they end up doing, the style of parenting that emerges will have a strong influence on the development of each of their children.

Four general styles of parenting have been observed, with each style influencing children in specific ways.

The ***"Authoritarian"*** parent is one who demands complete control over his child. While they may justify this approach in various ways, the underlying motivation is often a desire to control, or fear that something will happen to the child, or the belief that the child is incapable of taking care of himself. The child often responds with what appears to be an ideal nature. He is obedient, well-behaved, and easy to get along with. But often there is an unnoticed volcano growing beneath the surface because the child may not be allowed to express himself or grow naturally into an independent person. His good behavior may be caused by fear. This child may begin to make his own decisions as soon as he realizes his parents can't control him anymore. And his dependency on others to make decisions for him could put him in situations where he will "go along with the crowd" rather than use good judgment.

The ***"Autocratic"*** parent is similar to the authoritarian parent, but is characterized by a more impatient and demanding attitude. It's the "Do it yesterday" approach paired with inconsiderate and inconsistent parental control. Motives are often selfish and self-centered, expecting much but giving little to help the child grow to independence. The child may respond with submissive behavior, but not without a fight. He often looks sullen or morose—not a very pleasant personality to be around. He may even develop nervous tics or neurotic behavior and may be dependent on someone else to run his life. When he gets old enough, he may find very specific ways to assert his immature independence and intentionally hurt or embarrass his parents.

The ***"Indifferent"*** parent is not given this label because of a lack of love for his child. This parent may indeed care and be concerned for his child's welfare, but is so preoccupied with his own life pursuits that he has little time or energy to give to his growing offspring. He allows the child much freedom and little restraint. He gives little affection or signs of caring. Or, he periodically shows a lot of attention and then withdraws again to his own interests. The child almost appears to be raising himself. Depending on the quality of the environment he is living in at school, church, and home, and the character of other significant persons in his life, he may get along quite well. But often there is an underlying feeling of resentment and anger toward any proposed authority over his life—school, the law, anyone in supervision over him. He may be argumentative, a "fighter," a poor student, rebellious. If he doesn't have someone in his life he can relate to in a positive way, he may become delinquent.

The ***"Democratic"*** parent looks good on paper. Mom and Dad are willing to listen and discuss problems. They encourage the child to express his feelings about family relationships. They accept the child's right to make decisions about matters that involve him and trust him to make good judgments about his personal behavior. The child is usually friendly, basically cooperative, expressive, filled with good ideas, and motivated to *do* and to *be*. He is willing to face new challenges and even looks for them. However, the democratic parents who do not combine democracy with a clear understanding of a child's immaturity and the need for a certain degree of parental authority, could have trouble maintaining their own preferences regarding their child's activities through the teen years.

It is important that there is a good balance between control and autonomy, between warmth and a lack of concern, for the child to be balanced in his approach to life.

Obviously, the most effective style of parenting is one that helps free each individual child to become his own best person. At first it may seem simple to analyze and adjust a parenting style to our children's advantage. However, there's a catch! Parents are also caught in the bind of their *own* personhood, their relationship to one another in the marriage, and to possible contradictions in philosophies of discipline and child-rearing. In addition, the individual temperaments of our children cause us to react in different ways. We may use different patterns of parenting with each of our children.

Perhaps the greatest reason to be aware of parenting styles is to help us analyze our responses to each of our children, individually, and to discover how we may have been using a mode of interaction with one or several of our children that has not only been ineffective, but may have contributed to some of our problems. *It is never too late* to make changes. Especially if we can communicate our lack of understanding to that particular child, ask his forgiveness, and make a new start.

Scriptural Advice for Raising Our Children

The Scriptures give many suggestions for child-rearing. Unfortunately, some parents have misunderstood what they have read or been told, and have done damage to their children's psyche in the process. Some portions of biblical truth, taken out of context or without regard to *other* truths, can be misleading.

For example, one difficult passage of Scripture is Proverbs 23:13–14: "Do not withhold discipline from a child; if you punish them with the rod, they will not die. Punish them with the rod and save them from death" (NIV). Some well-meaning but ill-informed parents have actually made a parental practice of whipping their children regularly for the most minor of infractions because they earnestly believe it is God's will. These same parents are dismayed when their children finally grow old enough to fight back—in whatever way they can.

We can find the real meaning of that particular scriptural admonition when we read the context. The reluctant, or "detached," parent is admonished not to withhold discipline from the child. The parent has not been doing his job, and while discipline implies training and a correction of steps, it also implies that punishment may sometimes be necessary. The "rod" the passage refers to is the reed-like grass found so abundantly in the marshy places of Palestine. Like grandmother's "green stick," it could give a stinging reminder without bruising the body. Parents need to know that sometimes loving our children means giving them temporary pain. They also need to know and understand the difference between a loving step of correction and the harsh, emotional, judgmental bruising of the body *and* the spirit.

The Gift of the Parents' Faith

The most precious gift we can give our children is that of ourselves and our time. In Deuteronomy 6:5–9, God gives parents the formula for raising children who will be most likely to accept their parents' faith. "You (*mom and dad*) shall love the Lord your God with all your [mind and] heart. . . . And these words . . . shall be [first] in your [own] minds and hearts; [then] you shall whet and sharpen them so as to make them penetrate, and teach and impress them diligently upon the [minds and] hearts of your children" (vv. 5–7, italics added).

How do we "whet and sharpen" the words of faith and belief in God so as to make them penetrate into the depths of our children's hearts? The words *whet* and *sharpen* have some very appropriate meanings. *Whet,* among other things, means "to stimulate the appetite." It means to make our children want what we have. It also means "to kindle" or "to quicken"—to stir up action of some sort. Faith causes us to act in response to the truths we believe. The word *sharpen* challenges us to be clear and distinct in the example we set before our children—to be keen, eager, wide-awake, watchful, and vigilant in the ways we relate to our family.

It appears that our faith in God, as parents, must be more than a "hand-me-down." It must be active. But our actions must have words to go with them, because the next words in Deuteronomy tell us that we must "talk of them when you sit in your house and when you walk by the way, and when you lie down and when you rise up" (v. 7). Furthermore, our faith and belief must be obvious to all: "Bind them as a sign upon your hand, and they shall be as frontlets (forehead bands) between your eyes. And you shall write them upon the doorposts of your house and on your gates" (vv. 8–9).

Answering to God

But even then there are no guarantees. Deuteronomy goes on to give the warning: "Then beware lest you forget the Lord" (6:12). There are many Scriptures that give warning to willful and rebellious children. God, in His infinite love and sense of fair play, has given each of us the power of choice—the choice to love and serve Him, or *not*. We must recognize and accept the fact that our children have a choice as well. They will, each one individually, leave the comfortable place of parental authority and stand before God, alone, to make that decision. Our job as parents is not only to help them progress *toward* Him but also to avoid *hindering* them from establishing a one-on-one relationship with Christ as their Lord and Savior.

"Fathers, do not irritate and provoke your children to anger [do not exasperate them to resentment], but rear them [tenderly] in the training and discipline and the counsel and admonition of the

Lord" (Ephesians 6:4). (That goes for mothers, too.) Oh that we could all manage to daily live that Scripture in our relationships with our children! But we are also human. We have our bad days and good days. And some of those days are hard on our children.

Going Beyond the "Parenting" Verses

As parents, we must realize that *all* of Scripture is our source of life and counsel. Too often, we fail to understand that what God's Word says to us about relationships in general *also* applies to our children. For example, we could paraphrase Matthew 5:23–24: "When you come to church and remember that your child has any grievance against you, *leave the church* and go make peace with your child! Then come back to church and present yourself to God."

Matthew 18:15, paraphrased, might read: "If your child wrongs you, show him his fault, *between you and him alone.*"

Wise parenting is many things. But perhaps most important, it is a spirit of humility. We must be ready to admit our own shortcomings to our children. We need to ask their forgiveness when it is called for. We must be real people in all things. We must be ready to forgive our child, even if that child is not asking our forgiveness.

Our children need many things from us. They need our love, our acceptance, our careful discipline, and our forgiveness. Each of our children is a special gift from God. The gift needs a lot of tender care—sometimes more than we are prepared to give because of our own unmet needs and deficiencies in character.

Parent Pain

Sometimes we wonder: Why *this* child? Why *me,* Lord? We truly tried, but we just couldn't make it work. Maybe God made a mistake. Maybe *we* made a mistake. This child should never have been born.

Years ago, I sat in a group of people and cried inside when I heard a mother say, "We went through hell for eight years. The only relief we got was when he died."

Parents of wayward children often vacillate between wishing their child out of their lives and fearing he will leave them. There is no relief, only moments less painful than others.

We *do* ask the question "Why?" many times over. Sometimes we think we know why, which usually becomes guilt over some small, or large, thing we remember we did to that child in the process of his growing up. There are no easy human answers to the *why*. But there is an answer from God.

God Has a Plan

The Scriptures remind us over and over that God is in charge. Many parents can quote Romans 8:28 (KJV)—"And we know that all things work together for good . . ."—and do it frequently in the midst of their troubles. But in isolating that particular verse of Scripture, we miss the intended message. Yes, all things *do* work together for our good in the overall providential plan of God; and all things that happen in our lives *are* fitting into a plan that God ordained before the foundation of the earth. But what we miss is that in the working out of that plan, the "good" is for us to be molded into the very image and character of Jesus Christ—to share *inwardly* His likeness. That confirmation comes for us in verse 29: "For whom he did foreknow, he also did predestinate to be conformed to the image of his Son, that he might be the firstborn among many brethren" (KJV). The development of our *inward* character, the mind of Christ—the loving, accepting, forgiving spirit—seems to be best forged through painful experiences in which we are forced to face realities, to love, to accept, and to forgive.

God Shows Himself Strong in Our Weakness

There's another aspect that needs to be considered. When my own children were small, I had a lot of opinions about parents whose teenagers were "in trouble" all the time, or were just plain trouble. I have few opinions anymore. I have empathy, understanding, and a desire to ease their hurts and fears. I want to help them come victoriously through these experiences with a deepened trust in God and a more mature Christian character. The apostle Paul alludes to this idea in 2 Corinthians 12:6–7: "Should I desire to boast, I shall not be a witless braggart, for I shall be speaking the truth. But I abstain [from it] so that no one may form a higher estimate of me than [is justified by] what he sees in me or hears from me. And to keep me from being puffed up and too much elated by the exceeding greatness (preeminence) of these revelations, there was given me a thorn (a splinter) in the flesh, a messenger of Satan, to rack and buffet and harass me, to keep me from being excessively exalted." The circumstances are different, but the main issue is similar. Paul had a problem he couldn't deal with. There has been much speculation as to what his difficulty was, but that's not important. The important thing is God's answer to Paul's *why*.

Paul begged for release. Sound familiar? God replied, "My grace (My favor and loving-kindness and mercy) is enough for you [sufficient against any danger and enables you to bear the trouble manfully]; for My strength and power are made perfect (fulfilled and completed) and show themselves most effective in [your] weakness" (2 Corinthians 12:9). That was enough for Paul. But, I imagine, not without some struggle. He settled into the attitude of "when I am weak [in human strength], then am I [truly] strong (able, powerful in divine strength)" (v. 10).

Does this mean God planned these dreadful things for me and my child? No. But God allowed these things to happen that we might experience the truth of freedom and what it costs outside the will of God. And, He promises to be for us what we cannot be in our humanness. Through these experiences, we can come to know, unlike in any other way, what it means to rest in the peace of God.

Using Our Sorrows to Help Others

There's another reason for our agonizing experiences. Isaiah 61:1–3 speaks of Jesus and the ministry He was to bring—healing the brokenhearted, opening the prisons to proclaim liberty and freedom to physical and spiritual captives—a ministry of comfort, reconciliation, and restoration. Jesus ministers to us in our sorrow so that we might know how to minister to others in their sorrow. Second Corinthians 1:3–4 explains to us that God is the source of all comfort and encouragement. He consoles and comforts and encourages us in every trouble so that we may also be able to comfort others with the same kind of loving care we received from God.

Jesus in us, as parents, can reach out to those who are hurting. He assures us in John 14:12 that we will carry on His ministry and do even greater things because of the mystery of God's Holy Spirit within us. Jesus was, in a sense, limited in His earthly ministry. He touched lives where He was and on several occasions even where He *wasn't*. But the power of God's Spirit living and loving through His children, is multiplied, magnified, and limited only by our inability to see beyond our own personal tragedies.

God Knows What We Need to Grow

God knows what we need to become like Him. He knows what our *children* need to become like Him. He puts our individualities and uniqueness together in order to help us all become more like Him. The end purpose? "That they may be called oaks of righteousness . . . the planting of the Lord, *that He may be glorified*" (Isaiah 61:3, emphasis added).

Our failures become the tools for His miracles. Why *this* child in *this* family? Perhaps this is the only place this particular child can find roots that will eventually bring him back into God's family. There may be pain for a time. But there will also be a time of joy. Take courage, Mom and Dad. Resolve to take positive steps that will give your lives beauty and solidity that will draw that child back to you, and to God. Start now.

Something to Do

1. Start with a blank sheet of paper, one for each of your children. Write each child's name at the top of the page. Take at least fifteen minutes to center your thinking on each

individual child. Write words and phrases that come to your mind describing that child—personality characteristics, interests, character strengths, weaknesses, things that "bug" you, things that make you proud, things that scare you—be as thorough as you can be.

2. Turn the paper over, and again put the individual child's name at the top of the page. Take another fifteen minutes and zero in on how you deal with this child when he doesn't live up to your expectations. Think of a specific example when you were angry or upset and were not pleased with the results of your discipline. Think of another example when you were able to control your own emotions enough to feel you had accomplished something with this child. Can you own one of the parenting styles (outlined in this chapter), maybe reluctantly, because of some of the phrases you used to describe this child?

3. Pray. Ask God to give you wisdom to know how to deal with each child as an individual. If you recognize areas where you have been neglectful or overly rigid, or anything in between, ask God to make you aware of how you may have hurt this particular child and how you can regain his trust and respect.

4. Write a letter to each of your children. Tell them of your hopes and dreams for them. Tell them of your prayers for them. Explain what you have been doing in these exercises and ask them for forgiveness, if necessary. Remind them that you are not perfect and you know it. Remind them that you love them. Encourage them to be the best of who they were created to be—even if it may be very different from your own dreams for their future. Give them the awareness that you will accept them for who they are and who they choose to become. Hold on to that letter.

5. Invite each of your children out with you, alone. Share the contents of the letter. Be prepared for rejection, disinterest, even accusation. But also be prepared for tears of relief,

expressions of love and warmth, and promises. Remember, this is only a beginning. You may not get the response you hoped for. But you will clear the stage for God to work in that child's life with a freedom that may not have been there before. Be honest with your child. You may "backslide." You may *forget* in a moment of frustration and anger all of the good things you said you'd do or *not* do. Ask your child to be patient with you. Let him know that you want the best for him, and you want the best for your family. Maybe you can't all agree on what is best right now, and those areas of disagreement cause conflict. Be real. Be honest. Seek your child's respect. Most important, decide now that you will never quit. You will sacrificially love and be a parent to this child as long as it takes to get his life on track—and then forevermore.

Prayer

God, my Father, the perfect Father, the perfect Mother. Teach me to be more like you. Teach my child through me. And may this child come to know you and love you and serve you. Use his uniqueness to bring honor and praise to you. And use my uniqueness to bring honor and praise to you. Amen.

2 Getting to Know Your Adolescent

Most parents can remember enough of their own teenage years to be terrified at the thought of living with an adolescent! For the average inexperienced parent, unsure of what to expect and how to deal with it, these years can seem to go on and on, filled with the impossible pressure to be "wise and wonderful" at every step. Suddenly those previously controllable little kids *know* that Mom and Dad are uncertain about what to do and they take full advantage of it. But this period of your child's life is not as mysterious as you may think. There are a lot of normal experiences you can expect—both good and bad.

Teenage Behavior Is More Predictable Than You Think

I've been counseling parents and teens for a long time, but I still find myself surprised by the lack of understanding on both sides regarding what is normal and expected adolescent behavior. Often parents *promote* rebellious actions in their budding teenagers by refusing to loosen the reins enough to let their children experience the impact of some of their decisions. Meanwhile, some parents are too naïve to be aware of what's going on out in the real world and give their children way too much freedom to explore and experiment. In between these extremes is a vast sea of bewildered parental faces who want desperately to see their children grow up strong and wise and mature, but who don't know how to deal with the new world their children live in. They don't understand what is going on. They can't relate to the drug culture or the widely accepted free sexual activity among teenagers. They feel frustrated by the awareness that their child is growing up and away from them, and they fear they haven't done enough.

Some parents are guiltier than others of hanging on "too tight for too long." The reasons are good ones. They see the ugly things going on out there in the world and want to spare their children from the bad experiences that go along with the "pleasures of sin." For the compliant, easygoing, parent-pleasing child, this may create some sticky situations—maybe some tears or an angry confrontation or two, but life will go on.

For the independent, strong-willed, I'll-do-it-*my*-way child, life at home may become unbearable as parents are seen as the epitome of idiocy. And for a while, parents may realistically ask the question, "Will there be anything left after this is all over?"

What, Exactly *Is* Adolescence?

Everyone seems to agree as to when adolescence starts—at puberty, which begins around ages ten to twelve—but there is little agreement as to when it is over. There are several suggested ways to determine if your adolescent is "over the hump." But these ways lead to vastly different conclusions.

One identifying mark might be when your child becomes economically independent. He can make it on his own financially. She can pay her own bills, be responsible for her own keep—theoretically at least—and live under her own roof. Another sign might be when Mom and Dad are no longer legally responsible for the child's actions. At the age of eighteen, "adulthood" is reached in a strict legal sense—voting privileges, full-time employment status, marriage without consent of parents, and drinking are sanctioned in some states. Full civil rights are reached. In other places, some of these rights aren't granted until the twenty-first birthday.

A third possibility is that the child is no longer an adolescent when he becomes psychologically mature. That can mean many different things. Perhaps the bottom line is that he has to show good sense, demonstrate awareness of cause and effect, and be willing to assume responsibility for all his actions.

Social and traditional maturity are other signals that adolescence may be over. These are hard to measure and may vary from community to community.

A final marker of the end of adolescence is based on biological maturity, which can be measured to a degree but doesn't really signal anything except the completion of physical growth.

The point is adolescence is a period of growth in our children's lives. Physical growth marks the beginning and perhaps the ending, but it definitely also includes intellectual growth, spiritual and moral maturing, social functioning, and establishing oneself as an individual, responsible for one's own welfare.

The Teenager's New Awareness

That budding youth in your home is suddenly faced with a whole new concept of himself. For years he has been getting out of bed in the morning, dragging himself to the bathroom, where he's been forced to wash his face, comb his hair, and brush his teeth. Now he's beginning to notice there is a *person* in the mirror looking back at him. Maybe he likes this person. Maybe he doesn't. He's also beginning to notice that other persons in his life—schoolmates, friends, kids a little bit older—are expecting him to behave in certain ways and to *look* a certain way. Or at least he thinks so.

This young person who thought he had things figured out (with some exceptions) now is faced with changing ideas and new confrontations—with friends, with academic achievement, with parental authority, with drugs, sex, and other issues of social conduct.

It is important for this child to be popular. It is important that she feel good about herself. Her personal appearance takes on new significance. He wants to be an individual, which means conforming to *his* crowd and the rest of the teenage world. The adolescent is entering a time of life when fads are exciting, friends are forever, discomfort of any kind is intolerable, and being "cool" is the only way to be.

Trust is important to him. That sometimes involves a strange kind of loyalty that excludes parents and family and envelops what seems to be a totally unacceptable group of friends (at least to Mom and Dad).

If Mom and Dad have been fairly successful in teaching the basics of self-control during the first ten years, the second ten probably won't be much worse. But if not, there are some rocky times ahead.

You've probably heard the opening line of Charles Dickens' *A Tale of Two Cities*: "It was the best of times; it was the worst of times." That sentiment can be applied unsparingly to these years. They are the best because we see a whole person beginning to emerge and function. They are the worst because these pint-sized adults often behave as if they have learned absolutely nothing about civilized manners and decency.

Every Day Is a New Challenge

Adolescence is a time of rapid change. There are obvious physical changes going on before our eyes, but sometimes we forget what the onslaught of hormones is doing inside that child we knew so well just yesterday. Our children's bodies are becoming adult bodies—far more rapidly than Mom or Dad feel comfortable with. The sex drive is strong and frightens parents nearly out of their minds.

Emotions fed by those wacky hormones influence every move and every decision. Reason seems to go on vacation. Girls giggle. Boys stumble into things. Girls have thousands of secrets—which they tell everybody. Boys dream of being quarterback on the football team or performing some magnificent feat that will cause everybody to know just how wonderful they really are. Girls talk on the phone and/or text, until Dad's patience runs out.

The basic philosophy of most teenagers is: "I am immortal, invincible. Nothing can happen to me." This can lead to carelessness, testing the limits, exploration, peer pressure, or even deviant behavior. Most self-styled rebels (about 90 percent of all thirteen- to fifteen-year-olds!) share a common belief: Parents were invented to destroy the lives of teenagers and the world would be better off without them.

One of the most confusing things to parents about adolescence is the reactivation of impulses that had been under control for several years. Perhaps the most troublesome is the adolescent's apparent wish to receive immediate satisfaction of all desires, sometimes at any cost.

And yet deep down inside there is still that frightened little child we *do* know pretty well. He is afraid of his new freedom. He is anxious about his ability to really be "one of the guys." She's afraid the boys won't notice her. He's afraid the girls *will* notice him. They are panic-stricken that they might not measure up to the other kids. Our adolescents scream for independence at the top of their voices, but there is something inside them that also recognizes a need for outside authority in their lives.

Perfection and Dreams

There are a few other things about teenagers we ought to keep in mind. This is a time of life when idealism abounds. The adolescent sees the world in the way she *thinks* it should be. She believes perfection is possible. If she can't find it, she will often decide to provide it.

Often adolescents have not yet been jaded by experiences and disappointments. Their view of reality, covered as it is by this desire for perfection, gives them a fighting spirit. If they can find a cause worth the effort, they will give it the best they have.

On the one hand, this idealistic bent is great. But life is far from ideal, and adolescents have a tendency to reject those who fail to measure up to their standards: parents, school, the church, "the system," almost anything.

Emotionalism, although it can have a dark side, can be a positive force in the teenager's life. While seeming to contradict what was just written, your teenager will almost always be tenderly forgiving and accepting IF he is approached in the right way—and IF he FEELS like it!

They have dreams. All adolescents have dreams. Some of these dreams are practical, and while a little "idealistic," they can provide a framework for future life planning. Other dreams are "just for fun." Dreams can provide a real and necessary escape from the hurtful events of these tough and trying years. Or dreams can be shattered by thoughtless adults who see no reason for their teenager to waste good time lying on the couch, staring at the ceiling. This is tragic, for teenagers and adults who have ceased to dream are unhappy people.

Adults who are invited into a teenager's dreams should feel very fortunate. At the same time, parents should never feel left out or rejected because their child doesn't want them to share in their dream world. Yes, it hurts. But our children need room to explore their own inner world without having to give account for it. Moms and Dads can, and should, express interest while still leaving the adolescent's privacy intact.

For adolescents, loyalty is deeply felt. However, that loyalty is not always well placed. We parents sometimes wonder why our child is so loyal to that group of slovenly friends who are always on the edge of trouble and so disloyal to Mom, Dad, and the rest of the family. It doesn't make sense. Well, it does make sense to the teen who is finding his own place in the world. And it is a different place than ours. We need to keep this in mind when we feel replaced by what seems to be a poor substitute for a caring, stable family.

Ill-placed loyalty can have cruel consequences. When our idealistic teen has to deal with the crushing blow of a loyalty misused, he may develop the jaded attitude that sits on the shoulders of too many of us for too many years of our lives. Being "jaded" means wallowing in the dull disgust that comes from repeated disappointing experiences. This is sadly common among our youth.

It's Not All Bad

On the other hand, teenagers have a vast capacity for joy! They can take great pleasure in things. They can let it all go and show exuberance and enthusiasm that we "older ones" can only remember dimly.

They have an excitement for life that comes from discovering so many new things. Life is opening up all of its secrets. Our teenagers can bring a beautiful, uninhibited flair into our lives—if we will let go of our stuffiness.

Also, our children, who have been so focused on themselves for most of their lives, are beginning to feel a growing sense of responsibility toward others. This sense of responsibility, like their fierce loyalty, often displaces Mom and Dad and embraces others. Parents are hurt and dismayed. But maybe this means we've been doing our job; maybe this is a part of discovering what responsibility is.

Their creativity, meanwhile, is exploding. Teens will try things that adults would only wonder about—or perhaps never even think of! Sometimes this leads to fantastic results. But the very essence of adolescence can also put a damper on creativity, because some things are required that most teenagers are not prepared to give. Effective creativity requires a certain detachment, while at the same time being committed to the object of creativity. True creativity calls for a passionate feeling for the creative project while still having a proper respect for the "accepted" way of doing things. It also demands patience. Our adolescent is not altogether able to handle these things, and sometimes his creativity may be put to more "mischievous" uses.

Don't Look at Me—Look at Me, Please

While our adolescent is reaching out, being loyal, developing a sense of responsibility to others, he is, conversely, totally ego-centered. He believes that the whole world is preoccupied with him. "Everyone" is looking at him. "Everyone" is interested in him. "Everyone" is always after him! This is particularly true of the early teen years, but not untrue throughout the entire period of adolescence.

This feeling of being on display to the whole world brings about several different reactions in our teen. First, he spends his energies playing out his life to an imaginary audience. That audience is sometimes admiring and sometimes critical—whatever he decides based on how he feels about himself at the moment. It doesn't make any difference if the environment of our teenager is actually critical or not. The fear of criticism is enough. In his inexperienced youth, he has not yet learned to accept criticism in a positive way, and anything that suggests he is not OK is taken as unfriendly criticism.

The real tragedy to the adolescent, however, is not found in the act of criticism. It is the fear of being ignored. He would rather be criticized than not be important enough to be noticed at all.

Even though the adolescent is ego-centered, he nevertheless has a very fragile, very weak, ego-strength. This brings about a second type of reaction to the idea that "everyone" is involved in his life: He sometimes creates a "personal story" about himself that fills in the gaps for his feelings of inadequacy. This may lead to wild stories that the teen tells about himself, and wants to believe, and wants others to believe. Parents can either respond by saying they know he's lying (which is true), or fall into the trap of believing these stories and become panic-stricken.

How do we know what is truth and what is fiction? We don't. But we need to take the time to coolly go about learning as much of the truth as we can, either to relieve or confirm our fears. Then we need to try to help that child come to grips with the need that has created the lie; or, if the fantasy smacks of reality, we must find a way to work with the child to keep wild patterns from becoming a destructive force in his life.

As horror-stricken as we might be, or as deeply principled as we might feel, the loss of virginity, the delving into drugs and alcohol, the beginnings of delinquency or deviancy, are not the end of the world for our teen. On the other hand, the loss of communication with them, and hence our influence on them, *might* be.

We need to be able to see the problem for what it is, and the destructive potential it has, and remain in control of our own emotions. The truth, like it or not, is that losing parental influence is a great loss for your child. As much as pastors may care, as much as youth leaders may reach out, as much as the schoolteacher, the church, and the community feel responsible, the parent is the person most interested in the child and his welfare.

If we have lost our influence and know it, we must reach out to these same people and search for whatever help is available. There *are* others who can make a difference when we have lost our ability to reach our child. But, sadly, no one will care for them the way we do. We must not lose touch with them.

In God's Hands

There is always hope for the parent who has committed their teenager to God. Even when we have reached the absolute end of our ability to cope with a devastating situation, when it seems as though we must abandon them to whatever fate may await them because of their rebellion and disobedience, the Word of God gives us a hint of promise: "Leave your fatherless children; I will [do what is necessary to] preserve them alive" (Jeremiah 49:11). "Although my father and my mother have forsaken me, yet the Lord will take me up [adopt me as his child]" (Psalm 27:10). "I delivered . . . the fatherless and him who had none to help him" (Job 29:12).

Perhaps it is a stretch of the desperate heart to cling to these verses, admittedly clipped from context. But when the last strings of control have slipped through our parental fingers, we need to know God is there. When we know that even though we have not forsaken our child, he has stepped out from under the protection we are offering, these verses can give comfort only those who have experienced it can understand.

Foundational Learning Tasks

Our adolescent children are tuned in to the newness of life bursting about them. They are inexperienced. They lack the wisdom that comes over time. Their newfound freedom can be a place of growth and developing maturity, or it can be a place of fearful experimentation that may leave them devastated and weary of life before it has even begun. These important years are the foundation for their future. They need to develop disciplines and accomplish certain tasks that will serve them well in the years to come. As parents, we have the awesome responsibility to help them develop in these areas. Developmental theorist Robert Havighurst suggests several tasks our children must achieve before being launched on their own.[1]

Task One—Accept Themselves for Who They Are Physically

As our teenager adjusts to taking responsibility for his own life, one of the first jobs is to learn to accept his physical appearance. Although certain things can be changed, he must come to terms with the large nose, short stature, or big feet. Unfortunately, parents can do little to help. Maybe the best a parent can do is to avoid teasing or overemphasizing anything involving physical appearance. While giving advice and encouragement might be fruitful, it could also easily be taken negatively. Know your child and help where you can. If they ask for help, be ready to give it without lectures and an I-told-you-so response.

Some adolescents seem to have it all—beauty, brawn, or fully developed bodies before they know what to do with them. Parents need to help these children accept this kind of body in an appropriate way without undue pride or showing off.

I remember a pastor's wife who bought her daughter a white bikini when she entered junior high school—because she "had

1. Adapted from Robert J. Havighurst, *Developmental Tasks and Education*, 3rd ed. (New York: David McKay Co., 1972).

such a great body and shouldn't be embarrassed about it." How much better to have learned how to accept that lovely body as a gift from God to be shared with her future husband! That young lady had some struggles in her later teen years relating to her body. For girls, outward appearance and inner self-image are closely tied. "You look awful in that—" can be taken to mean, "*You* are awful." Many young people are struggling with an identity conflict and their bodies are often who they see themselves to be.

Task Two—Develop Healthy Relationships With the Opposite Sex

Second, this blossoming youth must learn how to form mature relationships with the opposite sex. One of the avenues for growth in this area is dating. In our present culture, dating has come to mean something entirely different than it meant a couple of generations ago. We have to be careful about the terms we use. In some circles, *dating* means "we are having sex." In other circles, the word *dating* has become obsolete.

Parents must decide early on, before the potential "dating" years, what the guidelines are going to be for their teenager and expect to be challenged, no matter what they decide.

Often the healthiest form of guy-girl interaction starts with group activities, where teens as a group plan entertainment together. Being involved in an active church youth group is an important part of surrounding your teenager with positive relationships and safe activities. But even in a youth group, parents need to be aware of what kind of adult supervision is in place.

Pairing off happens. And with the blatant sexual messages being tossed at our youth today, steady pairing off has potential trouble built in. It may be better to have a clear understanding with your teenager that you will not approve of an exclusive, steady relationship while they are in high school rather than wish you had been more vigilant after it is too late. Communicating this with your teen may not stop a relationship from happening, but when you have safe parameters in place, your child will have to decide either to honor them or defy them. At least they will know the boundaries, and hopefully you will have explained them clearly before the need arises.

Being involved with safe and fun activities in groups gives adolescents an opportunity to test their newfound male/female roles and also gives occasion to learn some of the expected social "niceties." On the other hand, one-on-one dating experiences can be a test of popularity, potentially leaving your teen with the feeling that "no one likes me because I'm so ugly."

Obviously one of the most important aspects of dating is the development of a love relationship that eventually leads to finding a mate. Hopefully that means marriage rather than choosing to "live together to see if it will work." Unfortunately, today too many couples choose to live together first.

Task Three—Develop an Awareness of Their Sexuality and Discover What That Means for Their Life

One of the sad things to have happened in our society is the blurring of, or even the attempt to eliminate, "roles" in life relationships. What does it mean to be "male," or "female"? Are men and women truly the same? Do the differences, if there are any, matter? An important task for the developing young adult is to make decisions about their own personal sexuality—their wholeness as male or female. They will eventually adopt a lifestyle based on what they are coming to believe about themselves. We hope that will be based on truth rather than society's confusing messages. No matter how much our culture tries to avoid them, male and female roles matter in relationships and in families. A young person who has difficulty accepting his or her own sexuality will feel and be maladjusted.

Task Four—Achieve Emotional Independence From Others, Assuming Responsibility for Oneself

It is important for an adolescent to achieve emotional independence from parents and other potentially controlling adults. One adolescent psychologist suggests that the steps involved are similar to steps of the bereavement process. First, the child must struggle to control the need to remain attached. It is hard for the adolescent to break away from the security of his childhood. It is also hard for *parents* to move into a position of no longer being needed by their child in the same kinds of ways. Next is the realization that separation has indeed taken place. The adolescent reaches a point where he knows there is no turning back. Assuming increasing responsibility for himself, he tests the previously accepted belief systems. He might experiment with some behaviors not acceptable to those previously in authority over him. Then the feelings associated with actual separation begin to surface—guilt, loss, depression. Slowly the young person begins to develop an understanding of what the parent-child relationship meant to him and makes attempts to provide those important things through other means. If he works through these steps satisfactorily, he begins to own his new identity and forms a new relationship with parents and other important adults. He may be eighteen when this happens. Or he may be thirty-five.

The target outcome is a blending of awareness, recognizing that the world is a place of interdependencies. Remaining too *in*dependent may cut him off from communication with persons important to his growth, but remaining *over*dependent ties him to someone else's control over his life.

Task Five—Gain a Work Ethic and Take Financial Responsibility

The goal of economic independence requires the emerging young adult to apply herself to the reality of work, and drudgery. This sounds harsh, but the reality of life is mastering the self-discipline to do work of the most undesirable nature and follow through to the end. The adolescent who does not have the assurance that he can go out into the hostile world and fend for himself financially will be continually knocking on someone's door for a handout.

Our parents and grandparents earned their first cents (not dollars!) picking apples or strawberries, weeding gardens, or shoveling manure. Many jobs of menial labor are denied our children today. Some may expect to be making "lots of money" when they get their first jobs. They are woefully ignorant of what it costs to live on their own. Parents need to give them accurate information and experiences.

Task Six—Prepare Themselves to Approach Marriage and Family or Accept Singleness

Before our children leave our homes to make it on their own, we hope they will have learned something of importance about marriage and family life. These things are likely not uppermost on their minds as they are winging their way out the door, but eventually this will become their most important consideration. Who they choose as a marriage partner and how they establish their families will be a large determiner of their future happiness and satisfaction. In spite of the debates in their social circles about marriage, living together, sexual freedom, experimentation, and whether or not to have children, a majority of young people still wants to get married and have a family.

Unfortunately, there is precious little training for this most important of human relationships, and divorce statistics reflect this. As parents, we have a responsibility to our children to help them develop a right perspective toward love and respect for one another. We have the privilege of living before our children the commitment and responsibilities we bear to each other in a marriage relationship. That's a tough task. At a time when parents are often facing their own marital crises, we find that it is crucial to be an example of good things to our youth.

Task Seven—Find His or Her Place in the Larger Society as a Contributing Citizen

Yet another task our emerging young adult must learn is how to be a responsible member of a larger society. This involves participation in the adult world and learning how to integrate one's personal life with the larger scope of life in the community and in the nation, and perhaps even the world. It is important for each youth to find a place of meaning for his life, and then put himself into a position of service and supportive care toward the environment, other people, and the planet.

Task Eight—Accept a Set of Moral Values That Becomes an Internalized Guide to Behavior

The final task in this list is that of acquiring a set of moral values that becomes an internalized guide to behavior. This is a long process, beginning at birth and bearing fruit during the maturation period, and taking firm root as the teenager moves into their adult place in the world. It is important that moms and dads proclaim, explain, and live the moral code they preach to their children. Our children will pick up on the roles we model for them. The question is: *What* will they pick up?

One definition of self-indulgence is "allowing in moderation what those who watch me can then excuse in excess." Because we are imperfect people, we will fail in our consistencies. It is inevitable. But the important lessons our children can learn from this are understanding, forgiveness, tolerance, and acceptance. Failure only remains failure when our parental attitude is too filled with pride to recognize and make right the trespasses against our children.

Beyond Havighurst's suggestions, there is a most important task for which Christian parents must take responsibility.

Foundational Task—Choosing His or Her Own Personal Dependence Upon God and Establishing an Adult Relationship With Him

The most important of all tasks is the fundamental choice each of our children must make to acknowledge their own personal dependence upon God and establish an adult relationship with Him. Too many parents look back to a four-year-old's sweet prayer to "invite Jesus into her heart" and insist that this child has always been a Christian. Moms and Dads need to know that adolescence brings a whole new understanding of everything, including one's belief and friendship with God.

Maybe this child *will* continue on in complete acceptance of all that has gone on before. On the other hand, maybe this child will suddenly think he has "outgrown" God because he never really, honestly understood what that relationship meant.

Whatever the case, Mom and Dad must step aside and place that child in direct responsibility to God. This is especially true if the child is making rebellious choices. He needs to understand that while he thinks he is fighting with Mom and Dad, he is truly rebelling against the authority of God in his life, and will be directly answerable to Him. God will not fail us, Mom and Dad. When we take our hands off, He has freedom to put *His* hands on, and in a far more effective way than we could ever accomplish.

Some ugly things might happen. Our teen must know that God is dealing with him directly. He needs to know that we are praying that God will use whatever means are necessary to bring him to his senses. If that child has refused parental authority, he has said, in effect, "I am ready to take care of myself. I am only responsible to me." Our response should be, "OK, but know that you will answer to God for your chosen actions. Make your peace with Him. We will be here when you want us."

"Letting go" is the most difficult thing a parent has to face. This will be covered more thoroughly in a later chapter.

The Bow, the Arrow, the Archer

Kahlil Gibran in his poem "On Children," from *The Prophet,* speaks poignantly of the growing gulf between parent and child. He reminds us that each of our children is unique. He implores us to recognize that we cannot compel our children to think as we think; nor can we seek to make them like ourselves. They each have their own place in the world of their future. He gives the beautiful illustration of the parent as the bow that sends forth the living arrow—their child. Holding the bow is the Master Archer, knowing the target destination of the arrow, loving both the arrow and the bow, and beseeching the bow to be glad in the bending. What a perfect picture for us to visualize. Each of our children is known and loved by God in a very special way. And so is each parent. At a time when we feel our children slipping away, it is consoling to know they are in Safe Hands.

As our child flies away like an arrow searching for its mark, finding his place in the world as God, the Archer, intends, let us remind ourselves that the stability of the bow, moms and dads, may be the crucial factor in finding the mark. That's the purpose of this book. The message of hope and help is centered on you, Mom and Dad. May God give you wisdom and determination as you work your way through these pages.

Something to Do

1. As parents, each of you separately write down on a piece of paper what you see as the most frightening and worrisome aspect of your teenager's life at this point. Compare your fears. Maybe you each fear entirely different things in this child's life. Talk about your fears. Can you *do* anything about them? The important thing in this exercise is to identify areas that both of you feel uneasy about and take steps toward action that may help. If you disagree on what to be concerned about, recognize that God has given moms and dads different points of view. Each is equally important in order to see the whole picture. Honor your partner's fear by giving it credence, even if it may seem irrational or unfounded.

2. Use a separate sheet of paper for each of the tasks the adolescent should be progressing through during this period of his life. Mom and Dad, together, discuss and write down how you feel your child is progressing in each of these tasks. Don't dwell on past failures. Write down specific, concrete

actions you can take. Together, choose the action that would be least threatening to your authority and to your child's attitude. Start now.

Task One: Accept themselves for who they are physically

Task Two: Develop healthy relationships with the opposite sex

Task Three: Develop an awareness of their sexuality and discover what that means for their life

Task Four: Achieve emotional independence from others, assuming responsibility for oneself

Task Five: Gain a work ethic and take financial responsibility

Task Six: Prepare themselves to approach marriage and family or accept singleness

Task Seven: Find his or her place in the larger society as a contributing citizen

Task Eight: Accept a set of moral values that becomes an internalized guide to behavior

Foundational Task: Choosing his or her own personal dependence upon God and establishing an adult relationship with Him

3. Pray. Bring your fears to God. Bring your feelings of failure to Him. Leave it all there. Ask for His wisdom as you proceed from here. Remember that God has made it very clear in His Word, "If any of you is deficient in wisdom, let him ask of the giving God [Who gives] to everyone liberally and ungrudgingly, without reproach or faultfinding, and it will be given him. Only it must be in faith that he asks, with no wavering" (James 1:5–6).

Do you feel your faith is lacking at this point? Tell God. "I do believe; help me overcome my unbelief!" (Mark 9:24 NIV). This is always a proper prayer and it is one He will honor.

Prayer

Father, God, you know the path my child must take. Help me not to hinder him on his way. Teach me how to teach this child to leave our home and find his place in the world. May I be humble enough to admit my weaknesses and when necessary to ask forgiveness. And may I be bold enough to stand strong for the beliefs and values I hold dear. Amen.

3 Moms and Dads, Husbands and Wives

Nationally known author, lecturer, and minister Charlie Shedd made the statement several years ago that the most favored children in the world are the ones whose parents love each other. He went on to say that he finally learned after many years of marriage that the greatest thing he could do for his children was to love their mother. It seems to be true that the level of satisfaction we feel as husband and wife often determines the kind of love we can give to our teenager.

It is hard to believe during those bliss-filled courting years and the delights of early marriage that there would ever be a time when these two lovers might be at each other's throats—either literally or figuratively. The perceived source of their irritation might be even more difficult to imagine—the products of their love, their children.

It is commonly understood that the three things most couples argue about are how to spend their money, anything concerning sex, and how to raise their children. The first two have a lot to do with the third. When those children become teenagers, money, sex, and "How did this happen to our child?" can become weapons to use against each other. Teenagers cost a lot of money. Teenagers suddenly know a whole lot more about sex than we are comfortable with, and there is living proof that we, maybe *you,* failed to do right by this child.

But the typical problems of marriage can be compounded by something else: exhaustion. If engaged couples could look into the future and see how many dirty dishes they would wash, how many socks they would launder, how many diapers they would change, and how many childish messes they would clean up, there might not be very many marriages! Similarly, if potential parents could get a preview of their children as self-centered, know-it-all teenagers, perhaps the population of the world would slowly work its way to zero.

But thank God, He has blessed us with temporary blindness and insanity during those lovely years when the sex urge is strong and love is all that matters. Later, as we move through the busyness of our children's childhood and the turmoil of the teen years, it's important to focus on the young adult who will emerge, and perhaps become our best friend.

Joy . . . and Stress

There are several particularly stressful periods in the life of a marriage. The first year together requires a number of important adjustments as a couple gets used to living with each other. There is the joyful stress of getting acquainted in a different kind of way than during courtship and engagement. There is the frustration of the irritating little habits, and maybe some big ones, that the husband and wife didn't know about until they were living together 24/7.

During this first year, couples have to make decisions about how time and money will be spent; they have to adjust to each other's sexual wants and expectations; they have to learn to live with a new set of relatives; they must decide what to do about having a family; they need to figure out how to handle each other's work and career desires—in other words, they need to get their lives "in sync."

If a couple doesn't discuss these important issues early in the marriage, or even before, they will lay a shaky foundation for future happiness and stress management.

Then the first child arrives. Life will never be the same again. No matter how eagerly they looked forward to the infant, no matter how excited they were about his arrival, they can never quite imagine the constant presence of a baby. No longer will husband and wife receive each other's undivided attention. There will be a steady energy drain. Needs and wants will surface that were never thought of before. The budget will be strained. The young couple, previously free to come and go, will now have to pre-plan every move.

Sometimes that first baby is a surprise and interrupts "the plan." My husband and I were college students who decided it made more sense to be married and finish school than to waste all of that time and energy living apart and trying to find time to be together. So we married, and nine and one-half months later we welcomed our first son into the world. Life changed. Fast. We had known each other since freshmen in high school, but were just getting to know each other as an engaged couple. Now we were parents, husband, wife, and college students, with both of us employed to pay for it all. Talk about stress. But that wasn't the end of it. Seventeen months later there was another son. Yes, we did know how it happened, but it happened anyway. We adjusted. We enjoyed our babies. We were proud of them. But we put off getting to know each other until he finished school and we started our "real life" four years after our wedding. We were committed to a lifetime together, but it all came together a little differently than we had planned. It was not easy, but we never questioned what we would do. We just did it.

Life becomes quite different with the new responsibility of a helpless, dependent little life. The ability to accept, adapt, enjoy, and move into a new arena of living will depend on the maturity level of each marriage partner and their personal willingness to learn to make life work for the family. I'm not sure we were at a high maturity level yet, but we knew what we had to do, and we forged ahead. After the first baby, subsequent babies only add a little more stress. If adjustments have been made with the first baby satisfactorily, it's just a little more of the same. But it is so important that the new mom and dad make time to acknowledge and notice one another. Marriages, just like infants, need to be nurtured.

Interestingly enough, a second round of inevitable stressors surface just when it would seem life is finally pulling itself together. The children are growing up, life has become more orderly, and finances are manageable. Surprisingly, success itself, in one way or another, becomes a "dark horse" stressor! Perhaps Dad is handling a little more responsibility at work. Mom may have gone back to work or is experiencing more satisfaction with her job or career. There is independence and prosperity. Or maybe dreams have been set aside or abandoned, and each marriage partner is thinking, *Is this all there is ever going to be?* Life may not be going as planned, or hoped.

Parents are busy running kids to this practice, that game, a birthday party, a church event. Mom and Dad are worn out, frazzled. Husband and wife have little time to notice each other beyond who will pick up who when, and what time the next game is. Can affection and love survive when each partner feels alone? When they feel like their only contribution to the family is the paycheck or the taxi service?

I remember a delightful young couple I worked with several years ago. They had four children and both had professional jobs. As the children reached this stage of life it was decided that Mom should take a leave from her work and manage the children's comings and goings and be a stable presence at home. Dad took on more hours—actually a second job using his professional expertise. He was rarely home during the evening hours to be with the family and worked every other weekend. Mom was feeling like a single parent and resenting it. He was feeling like he was less and less a part of the family. We spent many hours talking about what they really wanted for their family, and as a result they made some significant decisions. Mom went back to work part-time for a short period. They sold some of their "toys." They paid off a significant amount of their debt and cut their style of living dramatically. Dad quit his second job. I saw them several times over the next years in our small community, and they, each time, told me how much happier they and their children were and how little they missed what they thought they needed to be "happy." How easy it is to get caught up in the expectations of the world around us and lose sight of the things that are truly satisfying and important. This couple got it right, and their children received the benefit.

The third stressful period happens as the midlife years arrive. It is a time of reexamining one's direction and place in this world. A time of realizing that youth is fleeting and the physical body is not what it used to be. There may be anxieties, frustrations, a sudden lack of purpose, feelings of isolation, or a changing self-concept. There may be feelings of being trapped by life and circumstances. The whole idea of the aging process brings weariness, fatigue, or boredom.

Along with all this personal introspection come teenagers who pinpoint all of our failures, even if they are perfectly "normal." And if the teenager is at all rebellious, self-esteem and success can be destroyed. If we have been able to evaluate and grow through the previous stages of marriage and kids, we may be able to stumble our way successfully through this period as well. But midlife, menopause, and feelings of "is this all there will ever be?" can erode our best efforts to hold it together. Husbands and wives need to look at each other, and themselves, and remember they are partners, for better or worse. And better *is* coming. This is not the time to make hasty, or even deliberate, decisions that can change life forever. Now is the time to renew our commitment to our spouse and choose to keep doing the right things, believing the best is yet to come. Because the best *is* just around the corner.

"Me First" Thinking and the Possibility of Divorce

It used to be that Christian marriages were thought to be invariably stable and secure from the trauma of divorce. But today's Christian home is almost as likely to be hit by this event as the non-Christian home. Why? A number of years ago I was asked to speak to a church group of young married couples on the topic of "Why Do Christian Couples Divorce?" As I began to consider how to approach this topic, it occurred to me that there was only one reason, really, that divorce happens for any couple. One person in the marriage is not getting what they want. Maybe both.

Perhaps the Christian world has become far more colored and invaded by a worldly philosophy than we might like to admit. Perhaps the general attitude of "I must seek my own satisfaction and fulfillment at whatever cost" has filtered into our thinking. It is sadly rare today for a couple to do everything they can to save the marriage, or stay together for the sake of the children.

Perhaps we have forgotten or deliberately ignored the scriptural basis for marriage and become lost in the frantic desire for personal happiness. A definition of happiness that I heard many years ago says it all: "Happiness is what happens when happenstances happen to happen that happen to make me happy." According to that definition, my happiness comes from events outside myself. If I am looking to my spouse or to my children to make me happy, I am going to be disappointed. Especially when those children become teenagers!

God defines happiness differently. A look at the beatitudes in Matthew 5—which could also be called the "be-happy attitudes"—suggests we are happy when we are truly connected to God and seeking Him in our lives. Contentment, satisfaction, a growing relationship with God—these are the things that keep a marriage stable. But they are sometimes hard to hang on to.

I was asked by a friend to do some basic marriage counseling with her mentally challenged daughter and her new husband. As I tried to make this as simple as possible so they could understand, I made a list of five essential things for marriage to thrive. I have used these Five Rules for Marriage ever since with every couple I talk to.

Five Rules for Making Marriage Work

First—be truthful. Honesty is the foundation for trust. Little dishonesties, a small lie here and there, lead to bigger dishonesties down the road. Hiding things from our spouses because they would not be happy with our choices, planning and doing things they would not approve of without telling them—these things erode the foundation of a marriage. It cannot survive long with this kind of disrespect.

Second—be kind. Too often we treat the clerk at the check-out counter with much more kindness than we do our spouse. When did we decide that it was OK to be rude and short with the most important person in our world? Husbands and wives need to remember how good it feels to be treated with gentleness and thoughtfulness. Be the person you wish your spouse was.

Third—always be ready to forgive. Forgiveness, overlooking the irritating little foibles of our spouse, is a necessary part of our daily lives. Why? Because our spouses are overlooking so many of ours! None of us is perfect. That is almost an unnecessary statement. We know it's true. But somehow we easily forget our own annoying tendencies and habits—things that no one knows quite as well as our spouses do. When we continually point these out to one another to get the upper hand, what have we gained? Hurt. Anger. Defensiveness. A feeling of defeat. Instead, we should let these things go. Ignore them. Laugh about them (to ourselves). If there are big things that need to be forgiven, put them on the table. Confront them and talk about them. See a counselor. But don't let things pile up until you can't see over the top.

Fourth (this may be the most difficult of all)—***always be ready to say, "I was wrong, I am sorry, please forgive me."*** It is hard to take responsibility for our words and our behavior when we know they have irked someone, or when we realize we were dishonest or unkind or unforgiving. It is even harder to go directly to that person and confess our wrongs. Love your spouse enough to give him or her the honor of your humble spirit in acknowledging you should have behaved better than you did. Even if you don't feel you were wrong in what you believed or thought or wanted, if you were not respectful in the way you presented yourself, apologize for your behavior and your words.

Fifth—accept your spouse exactly where he or she is at this moment. What relief and what joy to know that the one who has professed to love you more than any other in this world accepts you as you are, with all the warts and uglies. Do that for your partner. Do that for each other.

But that doesn't mean you and your partner can't change. Acceptance without change can be depressing. ***Believe in each other***. Give your spouse room to grow. Commit to your own "growing and becoming." Decide to be each other's best reason for becoming a better person tomorrow than you are today.

"In Love" Becomes Love

The essence of love changes over the years. We enter into marriage as an emotional relationship between a man and a woman. We call it love. Often it could just as accurately be labeled "lust," with a good dose of "like." Is it realistic to believe, or even to hope, that this feeling can last a lifetime? We expect too much when we insist that the excitement and passion of newness and sexual exploration last forever.

It is inevitable that you will wake up one day, look at the person in the bed next to you, and say, "Who *are* you!" And then you will likely say, "Who am I?" The day will come when you don't like your spouse very much, for one reason or another. Is that the end? Or is that the beginning of really learning what love is all about? Will you continue to talk yourself into maintaining a relationship that is distant, but convenient, that doesn't "feel" as exciting as it once did? Will you walk through the years, smiling on the outside, but feeling dead on the inside? It will depend on how honest you are with yourself and how much you are willing to risk in order to see positive change happen in your marriage.

Here is a definition of love that takes us to our highest potential: "Love is being the best person I can be, so *you* can become the best person you can be." Instead of thinking about what your spouse doesn't do for you, think about what you can do for your spouse. The Golden Rule was not given to us for everyone except our marriage partner. Do unto your husband/wife what you would have them do unto you! Or, conversely, don't do to your spouse what you would not want done to you!

Love requires a certain amount of knowledge and awareness of the other person in order to function successfully. Love is an art. It is ever growing and changing. Love can be learned. Love is other-person centered. It is outgoing. It is first concerned for the joy, welfare, contentment, happiness, and peace of the person loved. There are no shortcuts to the process of love.

Our society is pervaded with the notion of romantic, exotic, sensual "love." While the perfection and sensuality of the emotion-filled experience seems utterly desirable, it fades rapidly in the nitty-gritty of daily living. Love lives in the hearts of imperfect human beings. True love can only exist when each spouse knows and accepts the imperfections of the other and makes a conscious choice to continue loving.

Seven Theses About Love

John Powell, in his classic *The Secret of Staying in Love,* gives seven theses about love that help give us a working description of that elusive relationship.[1]

First, **love is not a feeling.** He states that feelings are, of course, a part of love, but to base our decisions about love on feelings alone is to miss the joy of turning tinny tinsel into burnished gold. It takes time to weather the unpleasant emotions and the pains of submitting our wills to another, and to survive the hurts we carelessly do to one another. Love takes time to grow.

Second, he reminds us that **love is a decision, a commitment.** There was a time when you decided, before God and others, that this is the person you wanted to spend your life with. Remember that time and let it be the glue that holds you together during the energy-draining years of busyness, heartaches, and teenagers.

Powell's third thesis is that **love is unconditional.** To expect unconditional love from another human being is to expect the impossible. Only God gives us that kind of love. In coupling our

1. John Powell, *The Secret of Staying in Love* (Allen, TX: Thomas More Associates, 1995).

married love with the love of God, we can learn the effective love that covers a multitude of sins and still continues to grow.

Thesis four is that **love is forever.** When we commit to loving our partner for a lifetime, we give ourselves the opportunity to understand the complexity of love. If there are time conditions and circumstance conditions, standards that must be met, duties performed in order to keep love flowing, insecurity will be the result. When love is a lifetime decision and each partner knows it, there will be a commitment to growth, to working things out, to seeking and finding the highest degree of satisfaction within the relationship.

His fifth thesis is that **the commitment of love involves decisions, decisions, decisions.** Love does not just happen. You must consciously consider what your spouse wants and needs from you. It means you must sometimes be unselfish when you really want your own way. It means you might sometimes confront your partner in conflict in order to clear a misunderstanding or promote growth or forgiveness. It means taking time to notice your partner and continue to learn about him or her. Do you still *know* the person you are married to? Or has that person become a stranger because you have spent so much time focused on other things that you have neglected to make time to see the heart of the person you live with?

The sixth thesis is that **the essential gift of love is a sense of personal worth.** In a very real way, what we believe about ourselves is dependent on the significant others in our lives. If we are lucky, we will have grown to adulthood with a reasonable amount of self-esteem placed there by loving parents and friends. The sad truth, however, is that too many of us have a deep lack in this area. The relationship of love, within the bonds of marriage, has the capacity to restore, to heal, to renew, and to impart to our lagging spirit the vitality of positive self-esteem. And sadly, the marriage relationship also has the capacity to deal the final death blow to our fragile sense of self-worth. In being loved, we learn to love—not only another but ourselves as well.

Last of all, **love means the affirmation, not the possession, of the one loved.** Selfishness wraps the loved one in a cocoon that eventually brings death to the relationship. Love requires freeing your spouse to be their own best person, to pursue the things they love and dream about. Love sometimes requires giving up some of the things we think we love for a larger love. When we expect and demand certain things from our partner and refuse to be content unless those expectations are met, growing will cease. We cannot, do not, own one another, but we do *owe* one another. We owe the honor of respecting our partner's ideas and dreams. We owe our honest contribution to their thinking. We owe our partner the honor of listening to their contributions, objections, fears, and concerns. In the end, we owe one another the kind of love that does not smother, demand, or expect more than they can give.

When it comes to the line of "authority" in the home, there is no room for making demands or staunchly insisting that one has the God-given authority to make an important decision when the other is adamantly in disagreement. The Scriptures advocate mutual submission, one to another, in love. But even in "preferring one another," as in mutual submission, someone must take the lead in difficult decisions. Too often this becomes the place where bitterness takes root. A husband and wife must face those decisions—and they may involve their teenage child—with an attitude of listening to each other and praying for wisdom, maybe even seeking counsel from someone who can be more objective.

Benjamin Franklin once said, "Let the husband be glad to come home, and let the wife be sad to see him leave." Too many times it is the other way around. The last place he wants to be is back in that turmoil-filled household with his wife hurling blame at him. She can hardly wait till he leaves so there will be some modicum of peace.

Parents Aren't Perfect

What does your spouse want from you? What stands in the way of giving it? Pride? Anger? Embarrassment? Guilt? Selfishness? It is especially important to be aware of your spouse's needs during a time of crisis in the family. The continual hurt and feelings of defeat that are caused by a headstrong, rebellious child burrow deeply into the heart of each parent, and sometimes in very different ways.

Each parent goes through his own emotional tug-of-war as he examines every angry, irritable word he can remember speaking to this child. Each remembers the times he or she lost patience and used physical or verbal violence to try to control a situation. They think of the times when this child made special requests—often very reasonable ones—and these were denied, maybe for what seemed like good reasons at the time, but sometimes "just because."

Parents remember the inconsistency of their discipline. They wish they had done "this" differently, or had realized how important "that" was going to be later.

Parents suffer over their own lack of spiritual discipline and their failure to faithfully impart their own Christian beliefs and convictions to their children. Or they wish they hadn't been so fervent in their "preaching," turning children away from the church and from God.

Humans are excellent at digging into the furthest reaches of their being and rummaging up every possible reason for failure and guilt. But there is a limit to what we can take. And as each parent goes through the list of his own failures, he reaches a point where he can't handle the burden any longer. There must be someone else to blame. That handy someone else may be the parent-partner.

So we begin looking at the failure of our spouse. It feels good to get the focus off of ourselves for a while. There is always plenty of material for placing blame on them, too. All of those years living with another imperfect human being provide quite a backlog of experiences to remember.

Things we haven't thought of for years begin surfacing. If partners are wise, they will keep those things to themselves. If the other parent hasn't already thought of a particular incident, he doesn't need one more reminder of his failure to be all he should have been.

Human nature is funny—even when we know we are wrong, or have done less than right, and even if we might be willing to admit it if we think of it ourselves, we are not likely to accept criticism from someone else, especially from our spouse.

Any attempt to escape our own feelings of guilt by focusing blame on our spouse will only widen the gap that is developing. This may be true even if blame is only fixed in our own minds and never escapes through our mouths. Attitudes can also be read.

Take Responsibility

The truth is both parents are guilty. Both are to blame. On the other hand, both are also blameless. It is not possible to be a perfect parent or a perfect spouse. To be able to deal with our own humanness, and the proneness to failure in our spouse, is a first step toward rebuilding and renewing the love relationship that has been severely strained. Acceptance and love can be there again if there is determination and commitment.

Each parent needs to accept responsibility for their own words and behavior with this child. Accept it, deal with it, talk about it humbly with the parent-partner. Ask forgiveness from the one you want to love, and be loved by, above all others. Be honest in sharing your own failures to be what you have wanted to be as a parent. Ask your partner to pray for you and with you. This can be the beginning of an entirely new love relationship. Your marriage can grow in this time of upheaval and fear for your child. As Mom and Dad find each other anew, the home front is strengthened for the good of this child.

Focus on forgiving one another rather than trying to assign blame. Present a united front. Your child may not like it, but he will have to respect it. Many formerly rebellious young people have said that what eventually brought them to their senses was the knowledge that Mom and Dad loved them, and perhaps more important, they loved each other. This awareness gave that child a sense of security and rightness that spotlighted his behavior in such a way that it became repugnant to him.

Forgiveness, supportiveness, renewed commitment to the love relationship between husband and wife—these are essential ingredients for growth and stability during a time that could destroy a marriage.

Make Your Marriage a Worthy Example

Many marriages that die don't end up in divorce court. Some of them just keep up a respectable front while the stench of death becomes obvious to both marriage partners and to their errant teenagers. This isn't good enough. Not for Mom and Dad. Not for husband and wife. And certainly not for the hurting child. And it isn't good enough for the church community we live in, either. The world is too full of dead and dying marriages. Christian couples need to be aware of their responsibility to those around them to show the difference Jesus Christ can make in individual lives and within the life of a marriage.

For couples who want to see miracles happen in their marriage, they are there to be had. But they must take the focus off the rebelling teenager for a moment and place it on their marriage.

Something to Do

1. Take some time, each individually, to think about the things that are important to you. Write down five of those things, and consider why they are important. How are these things being worked out in your life, or are they woefully missing? Does your spouse really understand how and why these things are important? Talk about them together. Listen to what your spouse says about *his,* or *her,* important things, without interrupting or offering your opinion. Write a response to your spouse's list, without judgment and without criticism. What did you hear? What will you do to acknowledge these things and work with your partner to incorporate them more fully into your lives together?

2. Plan something special for the two of you. A dinner date at a nice restaurant? Overnight at a luxury hotel? A day together, doing something simple? Share your lists and responses with the promise that you will honestly discuss ways to address these important things and make them a part of your commitment to support each other. For each important thing on your partner's list, determine two things *you* will do to help make this happen.

3. Make a copy of the Five Rules for Marriage and post it on your refrigerator, maybe on the bathroom mirror, anywhere you will notice it and be reminded to "follow the rules."

4. "Husbands, love your wives" (Ephesians 5:25 NIV). Take the initiative in determining you are going to show "lovingness" to your wife, regardless of how you feel. Know that one of her most basic needs is to have a deep sense of your caring and affection toward her. Show her the small kindnesses and actions that let her know you want to rekindle the attraction that used to be so much a part of your attention to her. Underplay the sexual connotations. For years she has known how you behave when you want to have sex. Surprise her. Just be tender and loving without expecting anything in return. You may end up being the one who is surprised.

   Tell her you love her—in words. Too often, men seem to have no appreciation of what those three little words mean to a woman! A husband can go for months never uttering those words to his wife and never realizing how devastated she is becoming because she doesn't hear them. Read this and forever know: Your wife lives on the words *I love you*. Give them to her often. And give her reason to believe you mean them.

   Plan something enjoyable for the two of you to do together. Maybe it's something you know *she* would enjoy, but you avoid. Don't ask her if she would like to do it. Plan it and invite her to be your "date." She wants you to be thoughtful of her and show initiative in restoring your "togetherness."

5. "Wives, respect, defer to, honor, esteem, appreciate, admire, praise, be devoted to, deeply love, and enjoy your husband" (selected from 1 Peter 3:2). Wow! What man wouldn't fight to the death for a woman who loved him like that! Find ways to let your husband know you intend to care for him and love him. Remember, love is a decision to do and be your best for the one you chose to love. Your husband needs you to find things to praise and admire him for. Maybe it's been many years since you believed there was anything worth mentioning. There are a lot of good things about the man you married that you have likely taken for granted for many years. Let him know you are thinking about the reasons you married him, and tell him how much you appreciate and prize those things that make him a man you can be proud of. You may have let the irritations and frustrations of living with an imperfect human squeeze out of your mind the things other people notice about him. Look for the good things. Remember the strengths he has shown through the years and thank him for being who he is.

   Give him some special attentions you haven't thought of for a long time. Cook him something special—a favorite he thinks you have forgotten. Forget the diet for one evening. It really is true—men are impressed by the things we do for them, the caring we show by thinking of their simple pleasures. It may be very difficult to initiate or respond to sexual things because of deep hurts or resentments—it is much harder for a woman to put aside the angers and frustrations and be sexually responsive. But, often, doing the little things—a nice dinner, a favorite dessert, saying the right words, biting the tongue when sarcastic comments want to surface—eventually bring a real desire to please the man who shares your home and your bed.

   It has been said that a woman's basic need is for her husband's love, security, and protection, and a man's basic need is for his wife's admiration, respect, and praise. If this is true, you can't go wrong by attending to these things with your marriage partner.

6. "Do, or don't do, there is no *try*," is a famous quote from Yoda, of *Star Wars* fame. Do the things you know will bring new life to your marriage. Don't wait for your spouse to make the first move. There is nothing easy about approaching a spouse who seems hard and unyielding, and baring your soul for possible further hurt. But if the alternatives are either continuing in a relationship that is cool and unsatisfying or ending the marriage, there is relatively little to lose. Be the humble partner who is willing to take the first step.

   Even if only one partner is willing to believe that God can work a miracle in this marriage through his or her obedience to God's will, a miracle might very well happen. Do it.

Prayer

God of the impossible, God of the difficult, melt my heart and show me how to be the husband (or wife) that will bring out the best in my partner. Work a miracle in our marriage. Work a miracle in me. Amen.

What Parents Need vs. What Kids Need Equals Conflict

4

Parents' needs and teens' needs are much the same because human needs are much the same. But the expression of these needs differs with age, perspective, perception, and focus. Too many times, instead of making the effort to recognize and accept the differences in the way teens make their needs known, parents allow the differences to become the separation point between parent and child. Some of these differences are unreasonable. Some of them are silly, but become the issues that raise blood pressure. Some of these differences mark a truly important phase of life for the teenager.

It takes maturity to be able to support the needs of our loved ones when we can't understand what their problem is. And it takes patience to give them freedom to think differently and the security of our love while they are sorting things out.

This kind of selflessness is often missing in our family relationships. Sometimes we attempt to hide our fears and insecurities behind a spiritual façade. We won't speak of our needs even to our spouse. We have the false idea that to admit weakness or failure is to confess spiritual defeat. And we don't allow or accept "weakness" in our spouse, our children, our pastor, or our church family. By hiding behind a wall of pseudo-perfection, we cut off communication at a time when communication is possibly the only strand of life left to the family.

Abraham Maslow, a twentieth-century psychologist, defined the needs he believed a person must satisfy and arranged them in order of increasing importance. His theory of motivation emphasizes how important the realization of these needs is in bringing personal satisfaction to our lives. Parents and teenagers alike have inborn urges, according to Maslow. How they are satisfied reflects our different perspectives on life by virtue of age and experience.

While Maslow's theory is grounded in the basic essence of each level of human need and is not age-specific, the model he proposes provides some thought-provoking inferences in the area of parent-teen relationships. Using the basic outline of his "hierarchy of needs," the rest of this chapter will build on the psychological and emotional concepts that this hierarchy might suggest.

Physical Needs

After years of hard work, many parents of teenagers have accumulated some material possessions—a home, furnishings, entertainment equipment, computers, cell phones, maybe some fancy gadgets, a car or two. We appreciate what we have. And we might even get a little possessive about the things we own. Our physical needs have been and are being met. At this point in our lives a large piece of our security rests in the observable ability to meet our own needs for physiological comfort.

A teenager's attitude toward home and all of Mom's and Dad's belongings is also possessive. Our teen's need for food, shelter, and clothing are an accepted and expected way of life. We've always provided a bed for him to sleep in, perhaps a room of his own, good food, adequate up-to-date clothing, and possessions of his own that we never thought of having when we were teenagers. He may even be beginning to realize that the comfortable surroundings he has lived with and accepted as his "due" are not going to follow him when he leaves home and heads out into life on his own.

Conflict

What does this "possessiveness" look like in a teenager? He makes demands on the TV and the computer, walks around with music plugged into his ears, is on his cell phone constantly, slops all over the good furniture, balks at sharing in the upkeep of the house and yard, takes over the refrigerator and the bathroom, and brings in friends who do the same! He also expects unconditional use of the family car—at parental expense.

Parents get angry at this adult-sized kid who takes everything for granted and who has little appreciation for what it has cost to provide it all. In fact, this ungrateful child may show disdain and contempt for the quality or quantity of possessions in his home compared to the homes of his friends. He keeps on asking for more, and more, and more.

Resolution

Parents will usually have to make the biggest concessions. After all, winning every little battle is not nearly as important as winning the war. These suggestions will, hopefully, be tools to lessen the friction in the small things so that we can use our parental authority in the big things.

1. We, as parents, must maintain a sense of control. We need to expect and communicate that our teenagers have certain household responsibilities. We can be reasonable and willing to compromise in the use of the TV and the computer. However, parents must be careful not to sacrifice their own personal integrity in the process. Some of the programs our teens may want to watch, some of the music they may want to listen to, some of the stuff they may want to do on the computer, may

not only be objectionable but also be a poor influence or even outright dangerous. We should discourage them from these things or even forbid them. That won't necessarily stop them from doing these things elsewhere, but they will know where we stand and why. A word of caution: Know what you are talking about before condemning what you think is not OK. Do a little homework; watch, or listen with your teenager; and talk about it rationally with him. Have a reasonable and sound foundation for your convictions and concerns. Does he spend lots of time on the Internet? Monitor what he is doing—not as a nosy parent, but as a protector. Is his music too loud? Make a deal. When Mom and Dad go out, kids can turn up the volume (while considering the neighbors). It's the parent's home, too, and everyone needs to feel comfortable. Don't apologize for being "old and stodgy" (laugh about it). Remember, angry demands only push your teen further away.

2. Maintain a sense of humor. Try to see the funny side of your adolescent's behavior and your own response. Take time to think it through. Be willing to back down when you feel your temperature rising and realize you may have been the one who created the flare-up. Get in the habit of "saying it with a smile." Let your kids know you don't understand this "kooky" generation, but you'll live with it—as long as they, too, are reasonably sane and respectful.

3. Realize this is normal behavior. Teens cannot be expected to be terribly interested in keeping up with somebody else's possessions. They are hardly interested in keeping up with their own! But you are certainly within parental "rights" to remind them to take care of things around the house and clean up after themselves. As a parent, it's your duty to make sure they take responsibility for any problems their actions or lack of carefulness might cause, and to provide consequences for neglect or carelessness.

4. Recognize the scriptural truth "Do not store up for yourselves treasures on earth, where moth and rust destroy (*and*

> *teenagers take for granted*), and where thieves break in and steal. But store up for yourselves treasures in heaven. . . . For where your treasure is, there your heart will be also" (Matthew 6:19–21 NIV, words in italics added).
>
> We must never let the things we own become more important in practice than our family. While we need to consider the importance of our possessions, don't develop the mindset of protecting *things* from the family. Teach respect for property and maintenance and upkeep of possessions as good Christian stewardship. God has blessed us with these things to enjoy. We can be thankful and take proper care. Above all, we must be careful not to fall into the trap of loving things and using people. Things are to be used. People are to be loved.

Safety Needs

We live day to day, more or less consumed with the economics of living. We feel relatively safe and secure in the world we have produced for ourselves. We know if we take care of ourselves, we will be reasonably healthy—unless some unavoidable disease or accident comes upon us. We feel fairly confident that we can continue to provide financially for our families.

But we worry about inflation, joblessness, disease, accidents, drugs, and our kids—not necessarily in that order. We can handle our own safety needs, but what about our children? When they're home, we worry because they're not out, and when they're out, we wait for disaster.

What does safety mean to a teenager? Perhaps it means not being singled out in English class to read their composition. Perhaps it means being left alone in their room where they know nobody is going to say anything to embarrass them. Maybe it means taking a drink or two and driving everybody up and down the avenue, or taking a drag off the joint—because everyone else is doing it.

Teenagers often have unusual ideas about safety. They may be scared of nuclear war and industry-raised chickens, but the dangers of drugs, sex, and alcohol don't often occur to them. They may, theoretically, be concerned about physical safety—maybe even mental, emotional, and spiritual safety. But their major concerns are more immediate—what's happening right now.

Conflict

Mom and Dad are worried that this impulsive, carefree child might kill himself—or somebody else. They fear she could get carried away with drinking (teenage alcohol statistics are alarming). They're worried that he might get hooked on drugs (it's happening—not just "harmless" pot, but a whole new array of ways to get high). They hope she doesn't get pregnant or get married too young, or consider an abortion. These are life-changing choices that can destroy future plans. They can leave dreams unfulfilled.

We moms and dads start worrying the moment we know we're going to be parents, and we never quit! When these innocent babies become teenagers and we don't know much about what's going on anymore, we panic, or bury our heads in the sand.

Our safety needs are all wrapped up in our children's safety. We are afraid of the pain and anguish of losing a child. Our world crumbles just a little every time our children get hurt. Nothing is pleasant or safe when seemingly *uncontrollable things are happening.*

Resolution

1. Discuss with your partner what you can live with and what you cannot. Listen to your spouse's concerns. Make rules that are important to you and enforce them. Be realistic. Consider age and level of maturity. Keep the rules to a minimum for a good relationship.

2. Respect your child's privacy, but don't be afraid to check things out if you really suspect something dangerous may be happening. Tread carefully. Don't make ungrounded accusations or show a constantly suspicious attitude. Let your teen

know that trust is earned by being responsible. Let him know that while you may trust his intentions, you also understand the temptations and the problems that might keep him from always acting according to what he knows is right. That's why moms and dads make rules—to help their kids act according to their own best intentions. It's not a question of moms and dads trusting their teens. It is the teens trusting their moms and dads to love them enough to want to keep them safe.

3. Keep communicating. Let your teenager know you are interested in what's happening in his life. Be available at opportune times. When he starts talking, listen. Don't turn him off or tell him he doesn't know what he's talking about. This moment may never come again. And if you put him off, it won't be the same, even if you do pursue it later.

4. Trust God. "Unto You, O Lord, do I bring my life (*and my children*); O my God, I trust, lean on, rely on, and am confident in You. Let me not be put to shame or [my hope in You] be disappointed; let not my enemies triumph over me" (Psalm 25:1–2, words in italics added).

   We have a vicious enemy whose entire energy is aimed at destroying us and our children. God's reputation is at stake in us, and in our children. That does not exempt us from heartache and trouble, but it does give us grounds to call upon Him for help. And it gives us encouragement to follow *His* rules. If there is hope to be found, it is in God. Without Him, we may well have reason to be terrified.

   We can pray for our children to remain untainted by the world, and we should. But that really becomes their decision, not ours. In the end, we must: "Wait for the Lord; be strong and take heart and wait for the Lord" (Psalm 27:14 NIV).

   In addition, we must take advantage of every opportunity to remind our children of God's love and care—and His inescapable universal moral laws. Our teens need to have the awareness that they will never break God's laws. No matter what they choose to do, God's laws will still stand. But they will break *themselves* upon those laws if they choose to ignore them. They will reap what they sow. That is also a promise of God.

Most important, our children need to know that God is there to protect them. He is their safety.

The Need to Be Loved and to Belong

People need to love and be loved. This need can express itself most intimately and most satisfyingly within the family. Norm Wright, a biblical counselor, says that marriage and family can fulfill the basic human needs of loving and belonging, companionship, completeness, and communication.

Our families—our children—are extensions of our need for a closeness in companionship. We need from them a spirit of rapport and the satisfaction that comes from doing things together and from being together.

We see in our children, perhaps, the opportunity to make up for our own failures and lack of personal achievement. We tend to wrap a blanket of protection around them and say, in effect, "You are mine. I know what's good for you. I know what's bad for you. Do it my way. I've been around. I can save you a lot of heartache and trouble." This may be true. But our teens want to find it out for themselves.

Our need for love and belonging may be tied up in our adolescent. And if our marriage is not going well, there is an even greater need to hang on to our children, as they give us a sense of importance.

Our children have accepted parental love and caring as unthinkingly as they breathe and have life. They have belonged to the family unit. Without ever really examining it, or thinking much about it, they expect everything to always be there.

But now they need a different kind of approval. The love of Mom and Dad is not the kind of love to build their lives on. They need to establish a new world for themselves, and in so doing, they have to loosen the hold of their parents. They have to find out who else out there will love them, and whom *they* can love.

They are searching for something worth belonging to. Will it be a church youth group? a gang? Or will it be a group of scared loners who drown their fears together in booze, drugs, and sex? Maybe it will be that exclusive boyfriend or girlfriend who gives them a feeling of worth and special closeness.

They are looking beyond home and hearth for a sense of their own personal importance—whether in a group or with a special someone—to help meet that need.

They are expanding their world. They still need the security of home, family, Mom and Dad, but that's not enough. Their need for independence does not mean they have tossed their family out. More than ever, they need to feel the security of belonging to their family unit. They hang on to home with one hand while reaching for the stars with the other.

Conflict

Throughout this process parents often feel rejected. We used to be able to meet our child's needs for comfort, companionship, and approval. We provided the answers to perplexing questions and expected a little affection in return. We could do something for them and watch them delight in it. Now this withdrawing teen won't let us near. In fact, he goes to someone else. Boyfriends and girlfriends might take up all their time. And even when the adolescent is home, he may spend all his time in his room, alone, with his cell phone. Also, the smart mouth makes a regular appearance. There is back talk and sassiness, or sometimes they don't talk at all. Parents may even hear this dearly loved child say, "I hate you! I wish I'd never been born into this family!" Or they may read these words "accidentally" in a diary or a note to a friend.

Parents are hurt, and hurt brings anger. We lash out at our ungrateful offspring, trying to impress them with how important the family is, how important we all are to one another. And when our teen doesn't respond, we get resentful, bitter, and *we* close the door of communication. Our children go out to find their love and belonging *away* from us, rather than in *addition* to us.

Resolution

1. Affirm your love for your teen often—in word, in deed, and in gesture.
2. Give your adolescent a feeling of importance to the family unit. He should have responsibilities that *truly* contribute to the family welfare. Yes, that can mean emptying all the wastebaskets and the kitchen garbage as often as needed. It takes some thinking, and some planning, and some explanation, and consistent follow-through on the part of Mom and Dad.
3. Hang on to the older adolescent very loosely. Accept his reaching out beyond the family. Encourage your child to be a "friend-builder." Give him a feeling of responsibility in his friendships in order to develop awareness that *having* friends is also *being* a friend. Teach him that being a friend is helping someone else grow and become better for having known him.
4. Help your teenager to be discerning of other people, but encourage him not to display a judgmental attitude toward those who have different opinions and lifestyles from his own. Your parental example in avoiding judgment and criticism of his chosen friends is important. Our vehement disapproval only increases the need to prove that "this is a good relationship." Depending on the age and the maturity of the adolescent, we must walk carefully and prayerfully. Analyze *your* motives regarding his friends.
5. We must recognize that God did not give us our children to meet our need for love or to give us a sense of belonging. As we learn to treasure our love relationship with God, our Father, we will find less need to demand love from those around us.

Esteem Needs

A survey done several years ago found that a woman's number-one cause of depression is a lack of self-esteem. I wonder if that is not true of men also.

Many bestsellers have been written on the subject of building a positive self-image. We all need to be noticed, to be approved, to be useful, to be praised, and to be admired. A little honor here and there is a wonderful thing.

Our children are a grand source of "parental esteem builders." Who doesn't like to be told, "You have a beautiful daughter"; "Your son is such a good worker"; "I didn't know Jim was so talented"; "I hear Dale made the dean's list. Congratulations!"

We swell with pride and accept the praise as a personal tribute. We delight in the adulation of others. We want to be well thought of. It's important to be seen as successful in the eyes of *our* peers. *I am worth something. I have done something well.*

The teen also needs to feel the affirmation that he is an OK person. But there may not be much going for him at this point in his life. He is lacking in self-confidence. He feels that everyone's eyes are on him. He is constantly comparing himself with others to see how he measures up, and in his own eyes, he almost always falls short. He feels like he has to prove himself to his peers, his parents—to everyone.

Our teen needs the praise of his chosen companions. Most would probably opt for the praise of the "*in group*," but the majority of teens won't get it. So they realistically go for the group that gives them some reassurance that they may not be so bad after all. If she can't be the best athlete, the best musician, the best student, maybe she can be the best "boozer," the best "druggy," or the most sought after "date."

Or maybe he can just fade into the woodwork so nobody expects him to be the best of anything.

Most teens settle for being average and feel OK about it. But they need to know they are OK—and getting better.

Conflict

While parents need their children to affirm their parental worth and competence, our teens too often seem to be shouting the behavioral message: "Your whole life has been worthless, meaningless. You are a failure in the only important thing you had to do—be a good parent."

Parents are embarrassed among *their* peers—especially the ones who were fortunate enough to get the easygoing, cooperative children. These are the "other" parents who look at you with the slightly quizzical expression that says, "I really can't figure out what they did wrong. They *seem* like such nice people." When our children get in trouble or cause trouble, it becomes a personal defeat. Our bid for self-esteem is thwarted and kicked around until it is ragged.

And our children suffer, too. Parental accomplishments sometimes discourage and frighten our children. They may lose interest in trying. A highly successful parent may get frustrated with having a "lazy" kid, and the kid who is supposed to be a super-duper extension of the parent drops out of life.

Resolution

1. As parents, we individually must learn to accept our own weaknesses, our own failures, and our inabilities to be all that we may want to be. Then we must face the challenge of meeting those things head-on and working to change what we can.

2 We must learn that the highest praise we can receive, and the most pure self-esteem we can experience, comes only from our relationship with God.

3. We must accept our children for who they are, whether or not they live up to some expectation we have for them. We must give them approval for who they are presently and we must let them know it. That doesn't mean "dead-ending," and it doesn't mean approving the unacceptable. Quite the

contrary. It means we are willing to give that child room to grow and to "become."

Let's give our children the gift of believing in them—the trust that "with God, nothing is impossible," while at the same time helping them know they will always be precious to us, no matter what.

Need for Self-Actualization

Some parents, unfortunately, never grow up enough to be concerned with improving themselves. They remain hung up on the opinions of others and their own feelings and needs.

Within each of us is the bona fide desire to be more than we are—to grasp for that potential we suspect is there. We need to believe we are something more worthwhile and lasting than perhaps we have seen within ourselves up to this point. We want to become "aware," "fulfilled," "satisfied with the direction of my life."

True self-actualization is something that needs maturity to flower and grow, but it is a need God gives us from birth. It is the motivation to seek life's fulfillment in Him. Blaise Pascal, seventeenth-century mathematical genius and religious philosopher, said it well: "There is a God-shaped vacuum in the heart of man which cannot be filled by any created thing, but only by God, the Creator, made known through Jesus."

Maybe the teenager has an even keener sense of this idea of the need for personal achievement because his life is less cluttered than ours. In his idealism, he longs for that sense of who he is. The need cannot be filled easily, especially in the immaturity of youth. But seek it he will.

Conflict

In searching for "themselves," adolescents may end up pulling too hard against any ties that bind. They sometimes seem totally detached from the things Mom and Dad value. They are often lost in their own world of dreams and self-involvement and appear unreachable. They believe that the small store of knowledge and experiences they have accumulated is the culmination of the world's wisdom.

Meanwhile, parents have begun to settle with themselves. They have decided that they are all they will ever be, realistically, and their dreams of achievement, importance, and success are as complete as they can hope for. Perhaps frustration is setting in as hopes diminish. There may be disappointment that at life's halfway point, they finally know they will never be all they'd dreamed of becoming.

Maybe parents have decided to make a "last" effort to make life more meaningful—a change in jobs, more education, a move to a new neighborhood. Maybe there is marital discord as mates shift around within the confines of the marriage. Maybe there is separation, or divorce. Maybe these parents are searching for a more meaningful philosophical basis for their lives. Maybe they have made a first-time commitment to Christ, or renewed their Christian commitment.

All of these things, and more, can bring kids and parents just short of blows.

Resolution

1. Parents must learn the art of "hanging on loosely" and "letting go lightly." Or as Dr. James Dobson put it, "Hold on with an open hand." We have to give our child room to grow and to explore the inner person he is becoming. He must learn to accept responsibility for his actions and to live with the consequences of wrong decisions. He needs to experience the gratification of right decisions and good results. We need to help him ask the questions, "Who am I?" "Who do I want to become?" And then we need to help him discover that he can be whatever, whoever, he chooses, within certain limitations.
2. We must help our child find the Solid Rock to stand upon while he is searching for somewhere to "hang his hat." If he is not willing to commit himself to God at *this* point in his

search, we can provide the solidness of our own faith as a tie-in to the Truth. We can keep before this child the beauty of Jesus as He is seen in us. We must recognize that the world has some grand allurements, and none of them will pass our adolescent by—he will have to make choices. If he is wise, he will ask our help. If he chooses to do it all on his own, he may find himself in deep waters. We need to be there when the questions are asked, and we must provide good answers.

3. Parents must pursue their own personal growth, while carefully assessing the cost to their family. There will *not* always be time to follow one's dreams. What is best for the parent—*really* best—will usually be best for the children as well. In any event, when the children are gone, Mom and Dad will remain and will need to live with themselves and with each other.

4. Our proper and determined purpose, as parents, is found in the Scriptures: "That I may know Him . . . [progressively become more deeply and intimately acquainted with Him . . . understanding the wonders of His Person more strongly and more clearly]" (Philippians 3:10). Achieving this goal will take a lifetime, but if we do so we will provide a role model for our children that they will never be able to forget.

Something to Do

1. Each parent, write five things about your life, personally, that you feel good about—something you have achieved, who you are, or how your life has meaning. Share these things with each other, and add a few to each other's list. Remind yourselves you are still a work in progress. Determine to "keep on keeping on" in spite of disappointments and things that sidetrack.

2. Now each of you, list three things you had planned for your life when you were a teenager that never happened. Why didn't these things happen? Are you satisfied with the way things turned out? How have you settled with it? This is

an important reminder that youthful thinking isn't always practical, or that plans don't always happen, but we still need to remember how important these dreams were to you then. Now think about your teenager's dreams.

3. Settle on a list of parent-teenager guidelines for behavior and activities. Keep it short. Keep it neutral. Have a reasonable reason for each expectation. Then have a meeting with your teenager and discuss these guidelines, explaining why you believe these things are important. No negotiations. Explain consequences. No surprises.

4. Each parent, write ten things you want to see happen in your life in the years to come—education, travel, social activities, church life, your relationship with God. Share this list with each other and discuss the possibilities.

5. Invite your teenager to write a letter to you, his parents. What would he like to do after high school? Has he thought about more education or training? What kinds of things would he like to spend the next ten years of his life doing? Where might he see himself when he reaches your age, his parents? You could even offer to pay him to write it! Do not make any critical remarks or give any negative commentary on this letter. Just thank him for sharing it with you. Then pray.

6. Mom and Dad, read Philippians 3:7–14 together. Read it in different translations. Commit to knowing Christ, to growing in grace, to becoming the best you can be.

Prayer

Dear Father, thank you for all your provision for my life and my family. We have everything we need and a lot of what we want. Help us grow and become the best we can be as we seek to find all our needs met in you. Help us teach our children to know you and to love you so they, too, will find their needs, and wants, met in you. Amen.

Listen Here! Or Listen, *Hear* 5

It really doesn't matter how much you know about your teenager if you cannot communicate effectively with him or her.

Communication is the foundation of all relationships. We are always communicating something whenever we are involved with others. That communication may be enhancing our relationships, helping us understand one another more completely, or extending our influence and developing mutual trust. On the other hand, it may be creating an atmosphere of hostility, withdrawal, negative attitudes, and mistrust.

It takes two people for real communication to happen. It starts when someone desires that someone else know what he knows, or value what he values, or feel what he feels, or come to a decision he wants. Effective communication requires that each person is committed to giving and receiving information.

Communication is a way to motivate others to action. It can secure more understanding between persons. It can be a way to win acceptance by sharing who we are or what we think. It can be a way for someone to feel more secure as a person and to enjoy interactions with others.

For communication to be effective, the person who is sending the message must be willing to get into the experience of the one they are trying to reach. If the receiver of the message doesn't understand, communication stops or is distorted. Within the family there are many natural barriers to communication. For example, each family member tends to see each of the others in only one role—Mom, Dad, brother, sister. It doesn't matter what that person's position might be "out in the world" or how he is respected, loved, or looked up to by his friends and peers. In the family, he is still "the little kid" or "just mom" or "the old man." This doesn't leave much room for growth or change.

It's often easy to believe it doesn't really matter what we say, or even *if* we say anything at all. *I've grown up in this family with these people. They know me. They understand me. They will always know I didn't mean what I said, or they will be able to fill in the gaps and read between the lines.* We are often careless about providing the kind of information that promotes effective communication.

The truth is we can't assume anything concerning what is going on in the mind of another person. One of the main reasons for discord in families is simply that the consciously felt love and good intentions in the heart of family members are not *communicated* in such a way that they are recognized.

Parents and Children Live in Two Different Worlds

As our children reach adolescence, they begin experiencing changing thoughts and feelings that are totally new to them. It is difficult for them to express these changes in words or to discuss them intelligently with their parents. They may be questioning some of the beliefs and values they have previously accepted. They might be embarrassed, fearful, or confused about these tentative changes and don't want to be challenged by Mom and Dad—at least not yet.

They may begin to realize they have never really personally owned all of the "spiritual" thoughts that have been placed in their minds. While Sunday school, church, and youth meetings have been an integral part of their lives, these may have just been things to do because everybody did them and because Mom and Dad expected it. Now they really begin to notice that many of their friends and acquaintances are not hung up on church like they are. If their relationship to the church has been based on "everybody does it" and not on a personal relationship with Jesus Christ, they will begin pulling away because they suddenly realize "everybody doesn't do it," especially the cool kids they may be beginning to admire.

As parents, we need to understand that parents and teenagers live in two different worlds. We may even have been educated in two different schools of thought. They have been encouraged to question and analyze. We have been taught to accept and keep the questioning to a minimum. Questioning is not bad. It is valid and promotes growth. Often parents, however, view their child's questioning as a rejection of parental values and thinking. What our child may be saying, is, "I want to know what the truth really is. Help me." We need to have a proper balance between questioning and accepting. But the differences in our backgrounds may create a barrier in our communication.

Parents and teens see the world through different sets of eyes. To a great extent, our kids know the world through the media. They believe what they have been led to believe. Some of it is true. Some of it is highly distorted. Some of it is so idealistic that it's amusing, but it is truth to them as they perceive it at this time in their lives.

Parents see the world through the lens of what they have experienced and seen. We often have an amazing lack of information about reality, too. There is much room for error in both views of the world. We run our communication through the filter of our own biases, convictions, and prejudices, and sometimes we can't seem to reach each other.

Contradictions and Inconsistencies

Our children are often perplexed by what seem to be contradictory values. On the one hand, we teach our children to obey the rules, respect the laws of the land, and then we speed down the freeway at 80 miles per hour with one eye out for the state patrol. There may be other small things that seem unimportant to us. We might recognize the inconsistencies in our lives, but we have enough "perspective" to ignore them. Our kids don't. They see them and are confused. It is a hindrance to communication with our teens.

It seems unfair that the burden of effective communication should be placed squarely upon the parents' shoulders. But, unfair or not, that's where it is. Our teens may not want to communicate openly with us about all the things we want to know. Separation from parents is a desirable thing for them at this stage in their lives. Sometimes they purposefully blur communication to maintain a distance. They are discovering the treasure of being alone.

There are times when our teens do not want to be understood. They know that parents will not approve of their thoughts, their desired activities, or their behavior away from home. They have intentions that they are a little unsure of, perhaps even ashamed of or embarrassed about, and so they may deliberately misrepresent a situation. Some teens believe that while "confession is good for the soul it is bad for the reputation!" Especially where parents are concerned.

Parents must understand they cannot pry or force their teen into an honest, open discussion. So what is a parent to do? Is there no way to maintain rapport, an open channel that will keep us in the running for our child's affections and interest? Must we back out of his life just because he is saying by all of his actions that he doesn't want us to interfere with his "growing up and finding out"?

Far from it! There are many things a parent can do to keep communication open, even if the communication seems all one-way for a long time. There are things that will touch the most rebellious heart but will still give your teenager the space he needs for self-discovery and independence.

Effective Communication Is the Parent's Responsibility

Mom and Dad must commit to trying to understand what needs to be changed and to make an effort to discover new ways of communicating. They need to be willing to say and do things differently.

Parents also need to take note of the nonverbal ways they give messages to their kids that may be killing the effectiveness of the message even before it leaves the mouth. Also, they must learn to respond differently to irritating messages from their teen. Even if only one party is committed to change and works at it, very often the others will be drawn into it as well.

Parents need to be aware that their teens will behave and respond according to what they believe about themselves. They will live up to the labels that have been pinned on them and they have accepted. They have had thirteen years or more to develop their self-image—good or bad—and their communication with their parents will reflect the image they hold of themselves. This teenager will select from the parent's message just what he wants to hear and little more. If the message is not consistent with how he feels or believes about himself, it will not register.

For example, if he consistently thinks of himself as a "loser," the message that he is great, smart, or successful, will be a lie to his ears, and he will discard it. Words alone will not increase his good feelings about himself. In fact, they may increase his belief that he is no good and others are taunting him. Communication—effective communication—with your teen involves much more than mere words.

Perhaps the most important thing for parents to zero in on is the need for a high level of trust to be there in order to be heard. If teens believe they can trust their parents to be understanding, open-minded, fair, uncritical, and nonjudgmental, they are more likely to disclose themselves a little more fully. But keep in mind that the emotional relationship that exists between parents and children makes it difficult for very much objectivity, especially when the issues revolve around moral values and standards.

Parenting Style Affects Communication

There are several common ways parents lose the conversation battle with their teenagers. When we examine these closely, we can see how our kids can lose the real message we are trying to send.

One parenting style is to order or command our children to do something. Often we accompany these directions with warnings or threats. We may feel we are asking something reasonable, but in the mind of our teen, the message received is: "My feelings aren't important. They don't care what I want or think. They don't think I'm grown up enough to know what to do without being told, or that I have enough sense to do what's right." This may cause resentment, anger, hostility, or maybe even fear.

Some parents feel a desperate need to constantly give their children lectures on morality or to preach Christianity to them. Kids respond with feelings of resistance and defensiveness. They may feel guilty for the natural stirrings within their bodies, or their questions regarding God, the church, and all the things they once agreed with. Parents can lay a guilt trip on their teenager and attempt to hold him in line this way, but it won't work. Sooner or later, he will break loose and find his own source of REAL guilt, much to the consternation of the parents.

This style of parenting causes kids to hear parents saying, "You don't have enough intelligence to form your own opinions or to make good judgments or to hold any values that aren't constantly pushed at you. Listen to me. I have it all together. I know what's right. You don't."

Many parents are quick to criticize, disagree with, and blame their teen for his behavior or words, but are slow to give him praise and positive evaluations. They believe teenagers should just know when they have done well and parents shouldn't have to speak of it. So what the teen hears his parents saying is "You're no good. You can never do anything right. Your ideas are all stupid." The teen feels inferior, inadequate, unworthy, bad, angry, hassled, and shut out. Small wonder they are not open to hearing the messages the parent is trying to give.

Then, in frustration over the ever-widening gap between parent and child, parents sometimes even resort to name-calling and ridiculing. But teens know when parents are behaving like children.

If Mom and Dad's behavior and speech is immature, how can he trust them to be the wise parent he needs at this time in his life?

Some parents become desperate to know what's going on in their teen's life and begin to question and probe. The teen feels like he is under the bright lights in an interrogation room under severe cross-examination. *What do they want to know? How much should I tell them? How much trouble will I be in?* He feels threatened, mistrusted, misunderstood.

Sometimes parents forgo communication and just try to interpret their teen's actions for him. They analyze and make a diagnosis based on what little information they have. What they are telling their exposed, embarrassed teenager is: "I am wiser than you. I know all about you. I can read your innermost thoughts and feelings, and this is what they are." A parent's degree of accuracy may vary from right-on to nowhere-near, but the teen has little he can say to refute the prejudgment his parents have made.

But the most fatal mistake a mom or dad can make is to decide to give the escaping teen all of the freedom he seems to want. The parents may tell themselves they want to give the child room to grow, but more often than not they just don't know what to do and so they give up their responsibility for the situation. The teen may interpret this as a lack of interest in his life. He may feel rejected or not respected.

These are just some of the ways we, as parents, can block communication with our teenagers. Examining our own style of sending messages to them is a first step in making some corrections that may give us more influence with our children.

Once we have begun to look at the ineffective ways we deal with our teenagers, we can begin to take steps to help bridge the communication gap.

Learning to Listen

Sydney Harris is quoted in the book *Understanding Interpersonal Communication* as saying that in personal relationships, the only structures that can stand are *bridges,* not skyscrapers. When we focus on the relationship we want to have with our teen, instead of building our authority and importance *over* him, we will want to go a long way toward building that bridge.

An important aspect of this bridge-building is listening. Listening is not the same as hearing. Hearing is done with the ears, listening is done with the mind and the heart. It is a skill one can learn.

Listening with love and caring involves integrating physical, emotional, and intellectual inputs in a search for meaning and understanding. It is hard work to listen. It requires active commitment. It requires concentration. We must learn to pay attention to the message behind the words that are spoken.

One of the most important aspects of our listening communication with our teenager is the response they read in our facial expression, particularly in our eyes. The face communicates our emotions more accurately than anything else. Through our facial expressions, we tell our teen just what we think of the message he is giving us—whether we are judging or accepting. We show our level of interest or non-interest in what he has to say. We show how deeply involved we are in the conversation. We also demonstrate the amount of control we have over our own responses or reactions, and we show whether or not we are trying to understand what is coming from our child's heart.

Eye contact is vitally important. We can open or close the communication channels by the way we use our eyes during a conversation. If we are too uncomfortable to look our teen in the eye and express our interest through this form of contact, he will sense our uneasiness and feel less free to share important things with us. By refusing to meet eye to eye, a person is saying, "I'm not ready to really be open." Whether or not your teen is ready and feels comfortable with eye contact, Mom and Dad need to express their openness and caring by making as much eye contact as can be managed.

There are several other things to keep in mind in order to become a more effective listener. First, we must be *prepared* to listen. Our attention span and ability to concentrate on the message is directly related to our physical or mental condition at the time. If we know we are going to be involved in an important conversation, we should prepare ourselves mentally beforehand.

The times when we really wanted to have an intimate and serious conversation with our rebellious son, we took him to a neighborhood pizza place that was known for its quiet and easy atmosphere. The tables were relatively secluded from one another, the room was darkened, and there was a fireplace where a pleasant fire was always burning. It was a place where distractions from the family, the phone, and all the familiar things that surrounded our home environment could be eliminated. We had some good conversations, but in looking back, I fear we did more talking than listening.

In preparing to listen to our teenager, we need to anticipate where he is coming from—perhaps a place of anger, rebellion, resentment, or defensiveness—and determine in advance that we will not allow these attitudes to distract us from the message he is attempting to give.

Parents must know they need to *listen* and put aside the inclination to keep jumping in with comments, which will only cause their teenager to "clam up." Listening and understanding, or at least attempting to understand, will be beneficial for both parents and teen.

Beware of "red flag" words or phrases—words you know will cause a strong reaction in yourself when spoken from your teen's mouth. Determine beforehand that you will not allow yourself to react to superficial, testing comments.

Agreeing with everything your teenager says or *excusing* wrong thinking and letting it pass is *not* the same as *listening to his side and accepting his right to express himself*. If listening is done well, there will be opportunity to share your own thinking and make an attempt to influence your child. But it is almost guaranteed that without listening, any opportunity for positive influence will be gone.

Expect Conflict

When trying to find common ground for communicating with rebellious teenagers, parents are almost always working with conflict. It is helpful to be able to examine the kind of conflict you are dealing with in order to determine how best to handle it.

There are three basic kinds of conflict. Simple conflict is a situation in which we know what our teen wants and he knows what we want, and they are different. Neither side can have its own way and keep the peace. A second type of conflict involves ineffective communication. The two sides actually agree, but through unclear messages and presumptions, they assume they are in disagreement. The third kind of conflict develops when the persons in the disagreement become so emotionally involved that there is a threat to their egos. They become most concerned about saving face and protecting themselves.

Conflict is not a bad thing. We have been conditioned in our society, and especially within the church, to dislike and dread conflict. We avoid it as if it were evil. And, in fact, conflict *can* be destructive. But it is usually not the conflict itself that hurts people; it is the poor handling of the conflict.

Conflict and disagreements are an inevitable part of life. Wherever human differences and uniqueness meet, there is the possibility of disagreement. Conflict in the home, with teenagers, is almost a sure thing. Earl Nightingale once said on his radio program: "If a parent and teen are not at odds at least once a day there is something wrong with one, or both, of them!"

Maybe that sounds a little negative, and I'm not sure it *has* to be true. But conflict is a fact of life. We will certainly have bad moments with our teens, but we also have the ability to make personal choices. We can *choose* how we will handle the disagreements we encounter.

If we better understand what is producing the conflict situation, we may be able to control our own side of it. One thing that breeds conflict is the different attitudes that parents and teens bring to almost any given subject. As parents, we bring our own personal prejudices, biases, convictions, and thoughts to the encounter. And of course we see our teenager bringing his newly acquired contrary opinions.

These opinions may or may not have value. But that really isn't the point. The point is that both parents and teens become defensive, and sometimes the less sure one is of the truth of his position, the more vehemently he will fight for it. Parents who are trying desperately to keep lines of communication open need to make a concerted effort to be tolerant, understanding, and personally poised.

Too often, we jump to conclusions and rush to make a decision about something before we know all the facts. In not listening to and examining the messages that have been sent, we create our own lack of credibility and an atmosphere of mistrust. We are seen as unfair, biased, unreliable, uncaring, contradictory, and hostile to our teen's desires. Our hostility, or *perceived* hostility, triggers hostility from our teen, and the war is on.

Generally, there are three ways a person deals with conflict. There are *"eruptors,"* who enter a conflict gung ho and are determined to win at any cost. There are *withholders,* who are afraid of conflict. They avoid it at all cost, withdraw, or run away. And there are *confronters*. These people look at the situation, analyze it, and make an attempt to work through the problem until the differences are resolved. It may seem obvious that confronters have the better approach, but most parents do not deal with conflict in such a direct fashion.

How can parents manage conflict situations with a rebellious teenager and hope to bring satisfaction to both sides? The best, most honest, answer is that sometimes there is no way to resolve a conflict satisfactorily to both parent and teen. But there are always ways to work with a conflict situation that are more likely to produce the desired results.

Managing Conflict

The first step is for the parent to gain as much information as possible. What kind of conflict is this? Is it a real honest-to-goodness disagreement where we can clearly recognize the issue each side is fighting for? Or is there a lack of understanding and the conflict is merely because of garbled messages we have been sending one another? Has this become an ego struggle? Is each side fighting for personal authority, trying to defend *himself* rather than an issue that is of vital importance? Is it about looking good, or feeling justified?

Or is the goal to honestly do the right thing?

If the real issues can be identified at the outset, there will be much more wisdom available as the parent attempts to settle the argument.

The second step is for parents to get their own thinking in order. It is important to reestablish their own stability and sense of right and wrong. When the emotions become involved, it is difficult to see things clearly. It may be wise to get input from trusted friends or a pastor or family counselor. It is not weakness to admit we can't see clearly. It is mature and realistic.

Third, a parent needs to have a sense of independence in order to act freely in the conflict. He needs to avoid feeling pushed or rushed into action when he is unsure of what to do. It is important to take time to think and evaluate. The parent needs to have a sense of his own autonomy before God and have the freedom to place this child in His care, particularly if the rebellion seems unsolvable.

Lastly, knowing that conflict will come and preparing oneself for it will give parents more confidence to deal with it. It will help them to be less anxious about the outcome. They can plan in advance, together, what actions will be taken in certain circumstances. They can determine to speak their feelings in a non-threatening way. They can take responsibility for themselves and how they will respond. In trying to understand their teenager, the conflict may be greatly reduced.

Parents have to be flexible as they try to find solutions to the problems that come up with their teens. They should anticipate several possible outcomes and be willing to discard "solutions" that don't work, trying something else instead. If possible, parents should strive to find something equally acceptable to them and to their teen. Both parties may have to give a little. If the teen is unbending, and the parent cannot in good conscience give in to their child's desires, parents will have to use whatever authority is still available to them to maintain control. In this case the conflict will not be resolved. Perhaps escalation will occur. And there may even be a point at which parents must decide they can no longer compromise.

When Conflict Becomes Rebellion

At this point parents must be aware that the relationship may come to an end as an all-out war is declared by the teenager. All effective communication may seem to be blocked as open hostility invades the home. Parents might even feel the necessity to remove the child from the home because of his lack of respect for parental authority and the upheaval being caused in the family.

When there seems to be no way to communicate, when the child is completely intolerant of any parental reaching out, what can be done? Are we forced to play a waiting game and hope for reconciliation? Yes, we are. But there is more to it than that.

Your child needs to feel the strength of love that is tough enough to set limits, but tender enough to keep reaching out to the child in rebellion. If the child is still in the home, the icy silence or near-violent verbal abuse can be met with loving attitudes that refuse to respond in kind. In such situations, the best advice is never to miss an opportunity to keep your mouth shut! The parent must work at bringing down the barriers and not allowing one conflict to escalate into further irrelevant conflicts.

Never underestimate the value of physical expressions of your caring. While your teenager may resist your expressions of love through physical touch, he nevertheless needs it. Even when he is at his most unlovable, most untouchable moment, he is likely to respond positively *inside* to the light, brief touch on the arm or the shoulder—the touch that says, "I care about you. You are important to me." Keep it light. Keep it almost unnoticeable. But keep it up.

One of the most effective ways of keeping the communication channels from being stopped altogether is the occasional note or card. The note can be left on the pillow, taped on the door to his room, or placed on the bathroom mirror. It might be attached to the milk carton or the Coke can. Just a simple note, or a humorous or serious card, something that says, "I'm thinking of you. Sorry we're not talking right now, but I love you anyway." This note can reaffirm your belief in this young person—you know it's going to turn out OK. It can, and should, be quite informal, almost incidental—just to let him know you're still there and you haven't given up on him. It's an affirmation that you will be ready to receive him whenever he feels like making the move back.

For the teen that is outside of the home, the problem is a little more complicated. It can start, though, by communicating your love to your child when he leaves the home, letting him know that he is always welcome back—under conditions that you find acceptable to your standards and values.

If you know where he is living, an occasional note or card will keep you in touch. But the only real source of peace at this point is our constant communication with God. Placing the absent child in His keeping is probably the hardest thing a parent is called upon to do. But the effectiveness of your open, honest communication with God will be the key to your own source of stability and power.

Remember, there is no beginning or end to communication. All communication affects our relationships—for better or worse. We are constantly communicating with our children, and they with us. *What* we are communicating can be controlled. Make the decision to be a clear and concise communicator of love, caring, and understanding.

Three Biblical Principles of Communication

The Scriptures have some interesting things to say about communication. Ephesians 4:25 urges us to "put off falsehood and speak truthfully" (NIV). Ephesians 4:15 reminds us to speak the truth in *love*. I call this the STIL principle—*Speak Truth in Love*. Truth needs to be spoken, but if we can't find a way to say it lovingly, maybe we should wait until we can. First Peter 2:22–23 speaks of Jesus, who, when He was reviled and insulted, spoke not a word in His defense. First Peter 3:1 looks back to Jesus' example and tells wives, "In the same way . . . they may be won over *without words* by the behavior of their wives" (NIV, emphasis added). Peter is speaking to wives with unbelieving husbands, but the wisdom of this admonition can be applied to all relationships, especially with our children. Winning them over *without words.* This is the WOW principle—*With Out a Word.* Jesus admonished His followers to keep their words simple (Matthew 5:33–37). He was speaking of promises made and oaths sworn, but the application to general communication should not be missed—a simple *yes* or *no,* without elaboration. That would be the KISS principle—*Keep It Simple, Sweetie.* This would be good to think about in many conversations with your teenager. Speak truthfully. Know when to keep your words to yourself, and live rightly. Keep it simple.

Something to Do

1. Consider the last "conflict" communication you had with your teenager. What was the core issue being confronted? Was it a value, belief, or conviction being challenged? Was it a disrespectful attitude toward parental authority? Was it a request that turned into a demand?

   Was it resolved satisfactorily? Was there compromise? Or did one party exit the communication feeling frustrated or angry?

2. After reading this chapter, what might you have done differently to resolve this conflict? Go to your teenager; share with him your thoughts about communicating with each other more effectively. Apologize for not listening, not *hearing,* what he had to say. Express that you will attempt to do better in the future and you hope he will, too. Do not revisit the conflict at this time, but remind your teenager that whenever he is ready to talk about some of the issues you disagree about, you will listen. Remind him you might not agree, but you will listen and try to understand how he feels.

3. Take a few minutes to write down some of your disagreements, perceived hostilities, or conflicts of beliefs or parental standards of behavior. Consider why these things are important enough to communicate effectively to your teenager. Is a core spiritual or moral value involved? Or is the issue parental pride or an egotistical authority struggle? Your teenager probably knows the difference. It is important that you do, too.

4. Dig deeply within yourself and review the words you use with your teen. Examine your physical reactions to his words and actions toward you. Is your teen mirroring some of your behaviors (and words)? Determine to think before speaking. Catch yourself before rolling *your* eyes at your teen's words or slamming doors, or making impossible pronouncements regarding punishments or threats you cannot (maybe even *should* not) carry through. Humbly talk about these things *with* your teenager. If you become honest and vulnerable, maybe he can, too.

5. Make a list of the things you really want your child to *hear* from you. Make it short—five things of utmost importance. How are you doing in getting the message across? How can you do better?

Prayer

Father, you have taught us how to communicate with you. Help me be more faithful and honest in talking to you so that you can teach me how to communicate my love, and your love, to my beloved child. Amen.

Peer Pressure Goes Two Ways

6

We were standing in the hallway outside the courtroom. Everyone was angry. Our son had pleaded "not guilty" on the advice of his court-appointed attorney. We had talked with him prior to the hearing and it had been agreed that he would plead guilty and receive some special consideration from the court. Now we were all uncertain as to what to do.

But the thing that topped it all for me was the crew of "friends" who had come to support him in court that day—the friends who were constantly encouraging him to break curfew, getting him into drinking situations, providing a place for him to run to, and pulling him down with them.

There was the "friend" who had written the checks our son had cashed—five counts of forgery. There was the girl whose house was a refuge at all hours of the day and night—not just for him, but for a host of young guys and girls with nothing better to do than "bum around." There were four or five others—long-haired unkempt-looking kids, all with decidedly contemptuous attitudes toward what was going on that day.

I looked at these teenage children and felt my own contempt, my hot anger toward them, my disgust, even hate. I felt "righteously indignant," while at the same time feeling gnawing twinges of guilt and hypocrisy.

How can a Christian be satisfied to feel such ugly things for children? Where was my Christlike spirit of love and concern?

Love? Concern? For these "losers" who had dragged my child into the pit with them? How I hated *myself* for the feelings I couldn't escape. My desire was to be a professional counselor of youth. Here I stood, despising the very kids I wanted to help.

That's OK, I rationalized. They've hit *home*. I can't love and care for them when they've helped destroy the only things that really matter to me in this world.

Is that so? (Another part of me was butting in now.) Could I tell other parents to accept their children's friends, showing them care and understanding? Could I tell other parents to accept their own kids in failure like this? Is it possible to love "in spite of"? How would we know, unless we were forced to try?

Peer Influence

Peers—the persons of or near one's own age—have always been important to *every* age group. They are the persons who help us learn what behavior is expected of us. They give the clues that help us interact on a social level. They give us incentives to control our impulses, or the feelings of freedom to cast off our inhibitions and natural restraints. Our peers help us develop age-related skills and activities. They share similar problems, joys, and feelings, and direct us toward a lifestyle compatible with our needs.

The society we are living in has increased the importance of the peer group, especially among adolescents. Family ties are loose. Grandmas and grandpas may be thousands of miles away. Children may never meet aunts, uncles, and cousins, who fifty years ago provided a network of persons to "belong" to. Parents are working, engrossed in their own personal pursuits. Neighbors are not even recognized at the supermarket. Everything, including the church, is segregated neatly into age groups—and never shall they even potluck together!

Our teenagers are given far more opportunity to be with one another extensively than youth of past generations. They have less responsibility than their parents and grandparents had and a lot more free time. Their entrance into the adult world is delayed by many years of schooling in order for them to make a living—down the road.

The teen may love his parents and siblings, but at the same time feel hostile and separated from them. The world he is growing up in is far different from the one his parents knew as teenagers. And yet in many ways it is very much the same. It's hard—really hard—for kids to talk with their parents about the emotionally charged issues of moral values, standards, and cultural changes. It is not nearly as difficult to talk with their friends who are experiencing the same world.

It's realistic that our children should begin looking to their peers for guidance. These are the people who are going to make up their adult world soon. They need to have mutual understanding of what that world is going to look like.

Unfortunately, when parents think of peer groups, it is almost always in a negative way. Peer groups signal peer pressure. And in parents' eyes, peer pressure is *bad*.

Good relationships, on the other hand, seem to be taken for granted. The peer group plays an important role in helping the young individual become more independent, especially in three areas. First, the strong emotional ties to family are relaxed a little as the youth begins to establish bonds of love and support elsewhere. Second, the peer group helps the teenager gain skills and courage to make decisions about his behavior. Third, peer groups help the young person begin to think through his basic beliefs and establish his own standards based on his convictions.

The teenager who cannot find a peer group that accepts him as he is—or is willing to become—is a miserable human being. He needs this affirmation of his worth as a person. A warm, caring, non-exploitive friend or peer group can be an important handhold through the tunnel that leads from childhood to adulthood. Acceptance and belonging can play a crucial role in repairing or smoothing over hurts that linger from childhood.

But as we know too well, peer groups aren't always positive. We rightfully get concerned and upset when the relationships begin to look questionable, or when we see long-term childhood friendships beginning to take a frightening turn. Often we don't notice these "turns for the worse" until our child is too far into the friendship or group.

There can be problems—serious problems—if the adolescent's friends are bordering on delinquent behavior. It's important for parents to know who their children's friends are, and where they go together. A parent also needs to express feelings about particular peers. The wise parent will keep these kinds of comments to a minimum, however, since kids have a tendency to stand up for the underdog, and contradict the opinions of Mom and Dad—"just because."

Pressure to Conform

Sometimes, too, parents are appalled at their child's need to conform to their peers. They fail to recognize that conformity is part of the adolescent scene—and the *adult* scene, as well, if we look closely.

I remember my own irritation when my teenage daughter *had* to have a pair of jeans that bore a certain label. She was willing to do nearly anything to get a pair of those pants. As soon as the original dark blue coloring faded, however, the jeans were worthless. The price was obscene, but they only lasted about three washings! Why were these so important? Because EVERYBODY was wearing them!

I remember a pastor during those years, who insisted his son wear slacks and dress shoes to junior high school to set an example for other youth from his church. He set an example, all right. He was so rebellious by senior high school, the family moved out of town, partly to get their son away from his peers—a group he had chosen because they also expressed their anger and frustration at being forced to be different from their peers! By insisting that his son be different, the boy's dad alienated him from a possible relationship with friends who might not have been as potentially dangerous to his development.

Parents must recognize that their kids *need* to look like their friends—at least to an extent we can tolerate, considering modesty and decency. And sometimes we need to increase our tolerance level, remembering that "this too shall pass."

In allowing them some freedom in appearance, we can also encourage them to set a standard. The same daughter who had to have the expensive jeans in junior high, when in senior high, decided with a group of her friends to start a weekly dress-up day. They dressed to the hilt—nylon stockings, high heels, dresses—and they did it together. It was humorous to see the contrast from faded grubs on Monday to dresses and high heels on Tuesday! But it was *their* idea.

Know Your Child's Peers

Peer groups can be a reinforcing ally. There is not as big a disparity between parental values and adolescent values as we sometimes think. In fact, there is considerable overlap between standards of the two generations. We all have certain common backgrounds—especially if our children and their friends have been raised in a church environment and have been taught certain values growing up. It is true that our children have been strongly influenced by the electronic age, but there are many common threads of right and wrong that weave in and out of their growing lives. Peers *can* help reinforce parental values.

But when the peer group seems to play an unusually important role in the adolescent's life, it is often due to a lack of attention and concern from Mom and Dad. Parents should carefully examine the amount of quality time and attention given to their teenager. How much interest is shown in that young person's life? Do you have shared family activities?

If a teen seeks out a questionable peer group, either actively or by default, often it is because there is no rewarding parent-child relationship, or the parents' values may be inconsistent, unrealistic, hypocritical, or ill-informed. But sometimes the young person simply lacks self-confidence. He is not independent enough to act on his own.

Just like our own children, our children's friends need to feel loved, appreciated, and welcomed somewhere. Why not in *our* home? Are we willing to make our home the center of impromptu fun?—the overnight non-slumber parties and other special get-togethers? We need to be caring, friendly, and accepting of our children's friends. We may have the opportunity to have a considerable influence on someone else's adolescents just by liking them, listening to them, "incidentally" imparting our values to them, and making them a part of our family fun times. Our children's friends can become our allies rather than our foes.

But what happens when we suspect that our child's friends are influencing his life in troubling ways? After all, we do have certain standards and convictions. And we *are* expecting our children to be different from so many in this world. Is there anything we can do when we begin to fear the peer influence?

There just may be. It comes down to the bottom line of love and caring. Invite these questionable friends into your home so you can know a little bit about them. Show an interest. Perhaps your child won't feel comfortable having these "opposing sides" get together, but if he senses genuine concern, he may be more open than you think.

Make friendly comments to your child about his friends. Ask about their interests in non-threatening, non-accusatory ways. Seek information through kindness and concern.

If the friends do come into your home, show an honest and caring attitude toward them. Ask about their families. Don't be nosy or pushy, but get the point across that you care. Raise thoughtful, thought-provoking questions about activities and values. Listen while your teen and his friends give their opinions. Be careful not to make ill-grounded accusations against your teen's friends. If he finds himself having to defend them and himself to you, he will withdraw from you—to them.

When Peers Are a Problem

When you *do* have the facts about troubling behavior within your teen's peer group, confront your teen without accusation and without anger. This may take a lot of prayerful consideration, but the love and concern you show may make the difference.

It may be clear to us that we cannot accept some of our teen's friends. If our child chooses to retain these friendships, we must work at maintaining some kind of rapport, setting limits that we feel are essential, and forcing our child to make a decision. He may choose rebellion. We must prepare ourselves to face it.

Don't be afraid to stand firm on your convictions and fears. Discourage your teen from seeing certain persons or going to certain activities if you have reason to believe their plans involve something questionable.

When your teen has been confronted, his plans thwarted, and his chosen friendships denied, he will probably react in one of two ways. The first possibility is that he may obey simply because he doesn't know what else to do at this point—but usually not without a fight. There may be angry words, tears, violent behavior, or threats. There may be stony, ugly silence around the house for a time. But if Mom and Dad can keep their cool through this storm and show firm, consistent tough love, a major victory will have been won.

The second reaction is much more frightening. Your child may decide that he will not tolerate parental interference in his chosen lifestyle and will go into full-scale rebellion. His disobedience may be quiet and hidden, looking like full compliance with your wishes. Or all hell may break loose and you will find your family at war.

It is difficult to determine beforehand what kind of reaction to expect from your child. As a caring, loving parent who is struggling to maintain whatever control is still possible, it is vital that these decisions be grounded in prayer and scriptural principles. You must be prepared to face the worst reaction you can imagine. You can only do that when you are confident of your position before the Lord.

The only other alternative you have is to permit your child to be with persons and do things that scare you. If you feel strongly about specific situations and activities, be prepared to stand your ground.

Stand Firm, Have a Plan, See It Through

Having done all you can do, you must realize that you, as the parent, really have very little control of your teenager beyond a certain point—short of chaining him to the bedpost. If he decides to be disobedient after you have made your position clear, you must decide what you will do. You can place restrictions on his going and coming, considering that he or she may totally disregard what you say. You can take away cell phones, the keys to the car, the iPod, or whatever electronic device your teen treasures. You can ground him.

Most teens I talk to consider grounding a joke, or worse yet, a badge of honor. If you do ground your child, it needs to hurt somehow. It's funny how parents deal with their children. Even when they are behaving abominably, we balk at really "hurting" them. Grounding without "toys" can make a statement. Parents need to be prepared to monitor the grounding or it will not be effective. I had a good friend many years ago who had a teenage daughter near the age of mine. My friend worked many evenings, and her husband was a train conductor, gone for days at a time. Their daughter took full advantage of her parents' absence, and when her misdeeds were found out she was grounded and couldn't watch TV. My friend would come home from work and rush to the TV to see if it was warm (those were the old days), and if it was, the daughter was grounded, *again*. At one point she told me her daughter was grounded until she was thirty years old. Obviously, not a very effective means of discipline. Parents need to consider that there may be more effective ways to help their children come to terms with obedience.

Most important, we need to realize that we cannot force our will upon a child who will not heed us and who has the ability to do as he pleases. We can and should make it clear to the child that we are not giving our permission for his rebellious behavior. We must speak our mind, but still recognize our inability to control him if he chooses rebellion. This child needs to understand rebellion will cost him. Make your child aware you are placing him directly in the hands of God. He may make his own decisions, but he will be responsible to God for all of his actions and activities. And he will bear full responsibility for the consequences that result from his choices. More about this in a later chapter.

It is extremely difficult for parents to deal with this necessity. We love our children and don't want them to suffer. But somehow, through the wisdom and power of the Holy Spirit in our hearts, we must find the courage to let our children hurt for a little while so they can realize the seriousness of their rebellious ways.

Parents' Peers

Just as the teen's peer group is important and vital to feelings of self-worth, so the parents' peer group is important for the same reasons. We may have more respectable ways of displaying our dependence on the approval of our church friends or relatives, but we must be aware of the effect they have on us. Wanting their good will may cause us to be less than truthful about what is happening within the family. We want to be seen as competent, spiritually alive, and successful, in parenting as well as in other areas of life. Any deviation that indicates we have lost control embarrasses us, demeans us, and damages our influence.

When we begin to notice others looking at us with what we perceive to be judgment or pity, we may begin to retreat and cut ourselves off from those who could be most helpful to us. It is true that some persons, maybe even those we count as friends, seem to enjoy the predicaments of others and relish the idea that "they're not so great after all." A humbleness of spirit, a willingness to be open, and the wisdom of knowing when *not* to share are all part of maintaining the important, supportive relationships that will help you make your way through this difficult time.

Something to Do

1. Who are your teen's friends? List the names of several of the people your child regularly does things with. How well do you know these kids? Have you ever had them in your home? If not, why not? List things you know about each of these friends. What are their families like? What do you know about their parents' values and lifestyles that might have an effect on their child? Do you know anything about the way each of these friends think? Do you know what their personal standards are? Do you *like* them?

2. Talk to your teenager about these friends in a friendly, interested way. Ask him why he enjoys each of these friends. Chances are he hasn't thought about it much. Take the opportunity to discuss the specialness of friendships that help each person feel important and loved. Talk about how good it is to have friends that make you feel good about yourself and help you grow into a more mature person—ready to accept responsibility and be a helper.

3. If you feel that some or all of these friends are not good for your child at this point in his life, what alternatives can you offer? Are you prepared to get involved with providing some positive youth activities? Are you prepared to move into a new neighborhood, a new church, a new school, if the gang is so firmly entrenched that distance is the only possible solution?

4. Have you set firm guidelines for your child that he understands? Does he know the activities you will not approve of? Have you given good, biblical reasons? Or are you hiding behind the church? Be firm in your own standards. Decide what your bottom line of acceptance is and stick to it.

5. Are you prepared, spiritually, to live with active rebellion? Examine your own heart before the Lord. Seek counsel from your pastor or a mature Christian you respect. Find someone to stand with you in prayer for this child. If you have not been actively involved in a small group fellowship, such as a

Bible study, perhaps this is the time to get started. There is much power in united prayer. And you will need the support and love you can only receive from *your* peer group.

Prayer

God, you love each one of us with a perfect love. My love is so imperfect. Help me to see the unacceptable friends of my teenager the way you see them. Give me an awareness of their hurt and anger, and give me wisdom to respond to their needs. Give me the courage to reach out and invite these lonely children into my life so that they might have an adult in their lives who is trustworthy and who cares about them. Amen.

Kids Need Something to Do

7

Teenagers are funny. They can stay in bed until noon, lie around half the day talking on the phone, spend hours prone in front of the TV, and be too tired to set the table for dinner or take out the garbage.

Or they can be out until midnight, get up at 5:00 a.m. to go to the lake, water-ski, play ball all day, go skating, go to a movie until 1:00 a.m., and then complain vigorously that they never do anything and that they shouldn't have to be in so early! But the bottom line is, kids need to be active and involved in order to prosper.

Social Development and Relationships

When it comes to their social development, there are at least six needs young people have.

First, there is the need to establish caring, meaningful, satisfying relationships with others. Throughout childhood, our children have spent time with playmates who have shared common interests and activities, but they have not depended on these other children to give them emotional satisfaction. Now their need for close intimate friendships has become crucial. They are looking for friends who are loyal, trustworthy, and true—friends who will care about them and understand them. "Close" friends may come and go during early adolescence as everyone is seeking, with somewhat selfish motivations, to establish relationships. Girls are usually into more intimate, exclusive friendships than boys are, but as they grow older, they each desire the closeness and emotional satisfaction of having a special friend to relate to.

Second, they need to broaden their acquaintances and learn how to get along with many different kinds of people. Young people who have the opportunity to be involved with youth of different cultures and races have a distinct advantage in learning to be a part of the world in which they are growing up.

Third, the peer-sensitive adolescent needs to belong to a group. He will attempt to become part of a group he strongly admires. Social groups and clubs abound at the high school level, and if he can't fit into the group he admires, he will find a group that will accept him. As we've mentioned in an earlier chapter, sometimes that group borders on deviancy and causes parents and other adults much concern.

The relationship a teenager has with his parents will affect the strength of his need to conform to "the group." Good family communication and understanding will give the growing teen enough room to explore group friendships and still maintain a sense of individuality.

A fourth important need of adolescence is the development of pleasurable friendships with the opposite sex. This is often a painful process. The real or pseudo-antagonism between the sexes begins to melt away as biological changes occur, accompanied by emotions and awareness of the attractiveness of "the other kind."

Learning how to deal with the awkwardness, the embarrassment, and the "crushes" can be overwhelming. Most young people work their way through it and gradually become more sophisticated in their contacts. Group relationships begin to change into paired relationships, and these begin to deepen into real affection and romance. It's important for parents to be aware of how rapidly the pairing off may develop and intervene when necessary.

Fifth, there is the need to learn about, adopt, and practice dating patterns and skills that contribute to personal and social development, wise mate selection, and successful marriage. Adolescence is a relatively short period of time in a person's life. But during this time, many of the major decisions for a lifetime are made. Actions are taken that sometimes set the course for the remainder of one's life. It is extremely important that responsible adults provide supportive help and opportunities for the enhancement and development of these vital areas in the life of our youth.

The last need is to find an acceptable masculine or feminine role and to learn sex-appropriate behavior. Society decides how a male ought to look, how he ought to act, and the roles he should perform as a man. In a similar way, female roles are set forth. There have been considerable changes in this country relating to "roles" and behaviors in the last few decades. Adolescent boys and girls, with parental guidance, need to look carefully at these changing ideas and sort out what is valid and what is not.

The emphasis on male-female equality needs to be tempered with a mentality of equal, but *different*. We were created by God with certain characteristics suited for the roles we would fill within our families. When our children don't understand the responsibility of these roles, their future families may suffer. In addition, our culture's obsession with sexual behavior has blurred many gender lines for our youth. Confusion abounds. Understanding a little about hard-wired temperament may help parents and their teenagers see how temperament differences do not create *gender* identification. Society will always be changing, but God's Word is the stability that grounds us and our children.

Questionable Activities

Clearly, our teenagers need opportunities to make progress in each of these areas. A wide variety of social programming is important to meet the different levels of maturity of our growing teens. By the time most young people are in the ninth grade, they are anxious for opportunities to be with the opposite sex. There is a need for places with a positive atmosphere where they can gather and have good, informal fun.

There are some activities that certain parents are not comfortable with—activities in which a majority of the kids are participating. For example, some parents feel there is good reason to object to school dances and activity nights. Much of the time supervision and chaperones are lax, and alcohol and drugs may appear on the scene. For younger adolescents, parents are uptight about the "pairing off" that dancing initiates, and for older teens, parents worry about the sexual stimulation that it may bring—particularly for their boys.

If dancing is off-limits, and your child strongly objects to your rules, there may be some rough times ahead while you attempt to stand by your convictions and still keep your energetic youth occupied with enough social things to do. Teens that are denied access to an activity need to have the vacant spot filled with some other wholesome thing to do.

Movies are another source of concern for many parents. For example, a couple of generations ago, movies were taboo for committed Christians. Today, there is little difference between the PG-13 rated movies and the most objectionable movies of the '50s and '60s. Many Christian families don't seem to be concerned enough about the messages their children are getting from movies that are rated "suitable" for young eyes and ears—let alone their impressionable minds.

It is important for families to understand the rationale behind *all* visual entertainment and its effect on our youth. Some of the programs we watch in the privacy of our living rooms would have been considered objectionable a decade or two ago. We think nothing of them now because they are in our home. But what are they teaching our children?

Video games and television teach our children more than we might want them to know about war, evil, and sexual exploitation. Do we really pay attention to what is being planted in their minds? Or have we given up, and given in, to all the technology of this generation?

The important thing to teach our children is discernment about what they look at, what they read, and what they do. They need to understand that all of these things will have at least some subtle influence on the way they perceive life and the way they respond to various situations.

Some of the rebellion parents experience from their maturing adolescent may stem, at least in part, from the unmonitored TV and movie viewing their child has been involved in for many years. There are many good, educational, and entertaining movies. But there are also many movies that our children should be discouraged from seeing.

But if we take a stand against attending certain movies, what will take its place? Bowling? Today's youth may turn up their noses at such a thought! But even though it can be a good, clean, fun activity, in the right setting, too often the bowling alley has been taken over by the drinking, drug-using crowd or guys looking to pick up girls (or vice versa).

What about the neighborhood game room? Video games are everywhere, but many of them have inappropriate themes or images, and almost all of them are expensive. And do we really want our children constantly transfixed by computerized images, almost to the point of addiction?

Christian parents who are concerned about their child's moral and social development find themselves constantly saying no to request after request. What's a kid to do?

Joining the Herd

It's important that our young people have outlets for developing their social growth. In early adolescence, group activities are healthy opportunities to begin that tentative approach toward the opposite sex. If too many restrictions are put on these activities and we don't offer other enjoyable options to them, social growth may be hampered or one-on-one boy-girl relationships may be fostered too soon, before an adolescent knows how to handle such relationships.

When parents either overprotect or pamper a child, it can lead to a desire in the child to be noticed, even if negatively. If the parent insists on controlling his child's social life, the child may become dependent on his parents for his social satisfaction and have great difficulty relating to others his own age in their sphere of activities.

Sometimes delinquent or undesirable behavior develops because our teens have outgrown childish games, but no new and acceptable alternatives have taken their place. They don't have enough to do. Restless adolescents want to be with kids their own age, doing almost anything. Being part of whatever activities are going on is one way of finding social acceptance.

Psychologist to adolescents, J. Church, refers to the group life of adolescents as "herd-life." The herd gets together at the local hangout for food, drinks, and small talk. The herd goes joyriding in the car, to a movie, to a dance, or to hear a band play. They meet at the mall just to walk around or to sit and watch. To be part of the teen social scene, a kid has to join the herd and be with them. For the rebellious youth, the herd may assemble at whatever home or apartment is available on a Friday or Saturday night for alcohol, drugs, and sex. But sometimes your child just wants to be somewhere with someone who thinks like he does.

Kids need something to do. If parents deny them the activities most of their friends are involved in, they may rebel and do those things anyway—unless they have something else that interests them.

Extracurricular Activities

Extracurricular activities are often a safe, enjoyable way for kids to socialize with their peers. Encourage your teenager to be involved in life—sports, music, clubs, and other activities that build positive thinking and provide wholesome fun. Help them find things they will be interested in. If parents' lives are too full to be involved in helping their teenager explore their interests, they are too busy. Make time. Take them to things. Support their activities. Show up at concerts and games. Have social events in your home. Give them space to breathe and have privacy, but don't hesitate to monitor their activities. Let them know you are there, not to invade their lives, but to be sure they are safe. It's your job.

Family Activities Are Important

It may seem unreasonable to suggest that perhaps the family is the first place to look for activities to fill the adolescent's time, especially after spending so much time discussing his need to become somewhat independent from the family. But family recreation is important to the development of a young person.

Family recreation refreshes each member of the family—physically, mentally, and emotionally. It also helps develop each family member socially. Playing together as a family helps members form good relationships. It helps strengthen family ties. It can help break down the walls that often keep parents and children apart.

Remembering family times of fun and laughter sometimes eases the friction of household management—getting chores done, discipline needs, and communication. I have heard too many teenagers say over the years: "My family never does anything together. I wish we did." Remembering times of family togetherness and laughter can prick the heart of the most rebellious youth and make him long to experience that togetherness again with the good feelings of "belonging."

I remember a pastor years ago saying from the pulpit that he and his wife had decided to have a family night every week and nothing would deter them from it. He vehemently (tongue-in-cheek) said, "We are going to have fun together, whether they like it or not." I know those children today, now adults with families of their own. They fondly remember the movies and game nights with their family growing up, chuckling over their own teenage attitudes and expressing admiration for parents who would never give up.

Too many parents make the mistake of believing they don't have time to plan family activities. And they sadly assume their teenager isn't interested in doing things with the family. There is always time to do what we believe is important. If we become convinced that our family needs more time together to just have fun, we will make time for it. And while teenagers may balk at participating, secretly they are probably happy it is happening.

What can a family do together that will create lasting good memories? Short trips out of town provide needed changes of scenery. They are not always within the budget, but planning and prioritizing might provide the necessary funds. Camping trips for a weekend (with borrowed equipment, if necessary) can be fun if all members of the family enjoy that kind of activity. Longer family trips can be memorable, although it's important to keep in mind that too much togetherness in close quarters is not always a positive experience. But if parents can maintain a sense of humor and keep their cool in such situations, order can be restored—and even *these* memories become fond as time goes by.

It is not so important *what* the family does as *how* they do it. Be enthusiastic. Whatever it is that you choose to do, put your heart into it and expect that it will be fun. Buy or borrow books on family recreation and memory-building ideas. You don't have to be super creative. Use other people's ideas. Don't sacrifice the parent role to be a playmate, but don't superimpose the parent role on the activity and steal the fun from it. Enjoy your children as they are, for who they are. You might wish they were different. (They undoubtedly wish *you* were different!) It will take years for them to conquer their immaturities, so in the meantime allow them to be immature and crazy, within the bounds of appropriateness. You might be surprised at how much fun your children can be if they feel accepted and enjoyed.

Be the kind of person your children enjoy being with. Put aside the teaching, training, discipline, and punishment issues for the moment. Put the golden rule into action in your play activities. Do for and to them what you would want done to and for you. What you do with your children is important, but who you *are* is infinitely more important.

As the family sets aside time to play together, they may be forced to reprioritize their busy schedules. It's good to be reminded that this time will pass all too soon. Your children will grow up. You will never be able to recall these days and do them over. Now is the time to make the decisions that will help bring your family closer together.

The church is often guilty of planning so many away-from-home activities for each member of the family that there is scarcely a night left when everyone is at home. Again, parents who are too busy to spend time with their children are simply too busy. If it is true that much of what our children learn is "caught" rather than "taught," then we need to spend a lot of quality time with them to impart our values and beliefs. Our service to God must first begin within the family circle. Be careful to get your priorities in order.

Thousands of teenagers responding to a questionnaire in *McCall's* magazine several decades ago rated the most important quality in a father as "someone who spends time with us." Teenagers *do* want their parents to notice them and spend time with them.

Responsibilities at Home Help a Teenager Feel Needed

Another part of socializing with the family, and one that may not seem to fit into the area of a teen's relational needs, is that of having responsibilities in the home. It is not difficult to make a list of chores in and around the home that any teenager could do. The difficulty is in getting them to do them. One young man from a large family told me that his job at home was to "stay out of the way"!

Too often parents think of the hassle of getting their teenagers to do something they don't want to do and so they just do it themselves. "Move over, get out of the away. I'll do it myself." These are not good messages to give our children. Youth will always complain about their chores. Adults often expect their teenagers to "whistle while they work," even though Mom and Dad rarely do so themselves. Because teenagers do not do their tasks cheerfully or they may need to be prodded or because they look tortured and complain all the way through, parents may choose to do the jobs themselves to avoid the fuss. But without responsibilities around the home, it becomes difficult for the teen to feel needed in any positive, constructive way. A sense of belonging and commitment to the welfare of the family unit is nourished when adolescents have tasks to do and complete them.

When your child has completed his chores, be quick to say thank you and make positive comments about anything related to the chore. If something needs to be done differently, wait till the next time to instruct. If the job has been done poorly, empathize, and suggest that maybe *you* didn't give clear enough instructions. Give your teenager every opportunity to take pride in his work, even the way he takes out the garbage. Don't overlook sloppy, careless work, but don't attack the character of the child if a reprimand is needed.

The Electronic World of the Teenager

Today's teenager might find most of their social interaction in the privacy of their bedroom, via Facebook, Twitter, or various chat rooms. According to the Online Safety Site, 71 percent of teenagers have posted personal information online. They further indicate that 69 percent of teens receive personal messages from people they don't know, and more than half don't think there is anything unsafe about posting personal photos or information online, including some who see no problem with providing cell phone numbers or information about where they live.

Facebook currently is by far the most popular site for social interaction, but recent statistics show slowing growth, many teens finding the site "boring." Some indicated they were losing interest because their parents and other adults were too intrusive. Still, a large percentage of thirteen- to seventeen-year-olds spend many hours visiting their Facebook friends.

An article in the *Chicago Tribune* suggested parents join Facebook and become friends with their child, the motivation being twofold—it provides a window into the teen's world and helps keep her safe. Obviously, particularly for the younger teenager, joining Facebook or any other site should be a family decision. You should remind your teens of potential dangers, and remind them you will occasionally want to see what's going on for their safety, not because you want to pry into their lives.

One of the great needs of teenagers is to have a life of privacy apart from their parents. The Internet has provided that opportunity. It has also provided the opportunity for predators to invade their lives. It's the parents' responsibility to know what their teenager is doing online and who they are communicating with—for their own safety.

On the other hand, it's also important that parents with access to their teen's virtual world not intrude or attempt to become inappropriately "best buds," or make comments that might embarrass their teenager or their friends.

It's also important that there be an understanding of what is acceptable and what is not acceptable for your teenager to access online. Remind them that you know they can innocently end up on a bad site, but they need to know they can come to you for help if anything like this should occur. Also remind them that it can be harmful to the computer if they open up unknown messages or sites. All of this is to make certain any issues are addressed *before* they become a problem.

You, the parent, can put blocks on the network and require passwords and log-ins. And in so doing, you may initiate an attitude in your teen that lends to animosity, mistrust, and sneakiness. But that doesn't mean you should stop. How you approach this is important. Teens often know much more about up-to-date technology and are more gadget-savvy than their parents. If you are technologically deficient, ask your teen to show you what he knows. And find an adult who can back you up with the information you need.

The Internet, including Facebook, Twitter, MySpace, and YouTube, can be fun and entertaining for your teenager. But it can also be a dangerous place for predators and bullies to prey on your child. New social inventions are occurring all the time. One dies.

Another takes its place. Stay in touch with your teenager about what's going on when he's "plugged in."

Texting Is the Center of the Teenager's World

I grew up with manual typewriters, carbon paper, wall phones with party lines, and black and white TV. My grandchildren keep asking me, "When you were my age, did you have ________" (fill in the blank with anything kids take for granted today). My inevitable answer is no. They shake their heads in dismay. They cannot imagine a world where you couldn't constantly talk to your friends via cell phone. *Dial* a telephone number? What's that? *I*, on the other hand, cannot imagine how *they* can do it—texting—so swiftly, and so simply. I expect we will, in the near future, have an entirely new set of ailments involving frozen finger syndrome and carpal tunnel in places we didn't know had tunnels.

Four out of five teenagers in the United States carry a cell phone. The only thing a teenager rates as more important than his cell phone is his clothing, according to a Harris Interactive study. A majority of them say the cell phone is the key to their social life. The average teenage girl sends and receives over 4,000 texts per month, according to a recent Nielsen survey. That's more than six text messages *each hour* they are awake. Teen boys text less—a mere 2,500 per month, about four to five texts per waking hour. Those are averages. Most of us know some teenager whose text messages exceed the average by many more per day. Texting has become the number-one reason 43 percent of teens want cell phones, according to Nielsen. And they also *talk* on cell phones, averaging 646 minutes of talking on the phone per month, girls again outtalking boys: 753 minutes to 525 minutes.

Are parents to blame for purchasing unlimited texting for their teenager? Perhaps. After all, why limit the number of hours and minutes a child spends texting friends? Cell phones—talking and texting—are an important part of teens' communication with their friends. Parents need to know it is OK to give their teenager guidance and limits to the use of their cell phone.

Talk with your teenager. Let them know you understand how important these avenues of communication are to them. Inform them you want them to have these opportunities, but as in *everything,* moderation and responsibility are key. You may have to set guidelines that make sense given the degree of success your child is having in school, or how much texting and phone calls interfere with homework, sleep, and family interactions. Your child may need to be reminded of how rude it is to ignore others in favor of texting and talking.

Your teenager needs to be willing to allow parental access to their phone list, pictures exchanged, and even messages, if you are concerned about how your child's friends might be influencing your teen. There are websites that will help you unravel the shorthand jargon teens use in communicating with one another. Check these regularly. An example on a recent *Good Morning America* episode warns us that even the most innocent-looking message can contain frightening (to the parent) information. The practice of "sexting"—sending compromising pictures of oneself by cell phone—should give us insight into the lack of awareness teens have of the seriousness of some of their actions. Cell phones and Internet sites are not private. Messages are not secure. Any and all information posted can be retrieved by someone who knows how, and increasingly that means almost any teenager!

As teens get older, privacy becomes more of an issue, and parents have less ability to know what their child is doing with their electronic devices. A parent still has the option of monitoring the family computer or any computer operating on the family Internet access. Decide what rules are needed, and monitor what goes on. Remind your teenager that when he can afford to pay for his own Internet connection and his own cell phone, in his own home, he will have complete privacy—at least as far as Mom and Dad are concerned.

It should also be noted that parents have a wonderful option for managing teen behavior by trading hours/minutes of cell phone and computer time for reading, chores, educational pursuits, or any other kind of desired activities. As a consequence of ignoring parental rules, confiscating the cell phone or limiting access to the computer may carry power not thought possible in previous generations!

Teens Need to Drive

A driver's license is a tremendous responsibility. It is also a privilege. I am constantly amazed at parents who provide a vehicle exclusively for the use of their sixteen-year-old as soon as he gets his driver's license.

For many parents, it is a relief to have another driver in the overstressed "everybody has to be somewhere, *now*" family. Often this child is given freedom to drive himself and family members (most states do not allow teens to drive other teens before a certain age and driving experience). This usually works out fine—but not always.

Parents must think carefully before giving their teenager freedom with a 4,000 pound assault weapon. For most teens, driving means freedom, especially freedom to be with their friends. Whether they are driving within the limitations of their age and license may or may not enter into their thinking. Driving gives teens "something to do."

Unfortunately, statistics surrounding teenage driving and friends are alarming. According to the National Institute of Health, one in five sixteen-year-olds will be involved in a car crash within the first year of getting their license. SafeTeenDriving.org states that car crashes are the leading cause of death among sixteen- to nineteen-year-olds. The Rocky Mountain Insurance Information Association says that death rates for drivers increase with each additional passenger in the car and, tragically, for the passengers as well.

What this information tells us is that distractions, inexperience, and immaturity are lethal partners in teen driving. Cell phone use, texting while driving, alcohol and/or other drug impairment, coupled with the teen mindset of "it can't happen to me" are the leading causes of car crashes. Parents need to even out the odds as much as possible. Teens must learn to drive, but they need to learn how to do it safely. The first few years of driving need to be closely monitored by parents.

An article appearing on DriveHomeSafe.com encourages parents to put together a Teen Driver's Contract with their teen. If you suspect your teen is driving irresponsibly, talking or texting on a cell phone (yes, texting—teens are quite proficient at doing this), speeding, or driving friends around even though it is not legal, have a conversation. Lay down the rules for safe driving, especially in the first eighteen months of new driver experience. Sadly, experience is sometimes a very good teacher. Accidents that happen in a moment of time, possibly injuring or killing friends, will follow this child for a lifetime, if he survives. Protect your child.

Also, let your teenager know he bears some financial responsibility for the safety and upkeep of the vehicle he drives. Maybe that means purchasing gas, changing the oil, paying for part of the insurance, or paying for any damage to the vehicle that comes from irresponsible behavior. Certain "accidental accidents" that are just part of the learning process might be overlooked, or the costs can be shared.

Teenagers who are shutting their parents out of their lives and who are behaving badly should not have the privilege of driving. That doesn't mean they *won't* drive without permission, but the parent has the responsibility of not funding driver's education, not allowing use of the family car, and not encouraging their teenager to purchase their own vehicle should they have the money to do so.

Most teenagers want to drive. Parents have the responsibility and the power to protect their children, and the community at large, by making wise decisions about this important aspect of their teenager's life.

The Church

The church we choose to become a part of will have a vital and undeniable influence on every member of our family. The church has a tremendous capacity to help both the family and our emerging adolescent. Conversely, it is possible for the atmosphere of the church to be detrimental to the growth of the young person and the family as well.

The church can provide a place where truth can be presented across the generations. As parents and children sit together listening to the same message, they may have different responses, but if parents will seek to have conversations about what they heard in church, they may get insights into how their children are thinking. It's possible they'll hear that their children are tuned out completely. That is important to know. The parent might consider offering an incentive for "answers" to specific questions gleaned from the Sunday morning message—extra game time, television time, maybe even money! It's possible your teen might consider listening in order to pocket some change. And he may hear something that will stick.

The church can provide a supportive extension of the family's values. This may be the only place in the teenager's world (aside from the family) that he hears a message that provides a restraining check on questionable activities. The church family, including youth leaders your teen likes and respects, can provide listening ears and counsel—someone to talk to besides Mom and Dad.

The Church Provides Opportunities for Social Growth and Service to Others

The social climate the church provides can be a place for the teen to find "something to do." It is important that the church community understands their role in providing positive and safe activities for its youth. For the teenager who feels he doesn't fit in with any group at school, he may find his place of social acceptance and belonging within the church.

The church can provide young people an opportunity to serve others and find a social conscience. Many churches plan short-term mission trips where the teen can experience firsthand some of the tremendous needs of the world we live in. Sacrifice whatever you have to in order to give your teenager such an opportunity.

Difficult Choices

If the church can be such an important part of our teenager's growing up experience, what is a parent to do when their child begins rebelling against attending services or youth activities?

First, the parent needs to examine what their particular church has to offer. One author suggests parents ask the question: "Is your church still breathing?" Is there a functioning youth group? Are the youth leaders "in tune" with adolescent thinking and wants? Does the church truly preach the gospel and biblical truth? Is this church too legalistic? Too liberal? Is it a small congregation with very few young people? Are *you,* the parent, bored with services but still attending out of habit? Is this church alive and growing, not necessarily in numbers but in spirit? Is it a healthy environment for young people?

It is important to be loyal to your church. It shows dedication and conviction to be supportive of the church family you may have been part of for many years. But to stay in an unhealthy environment out of obligation may be detrimental to your children. Many dedicated parents stay year after year in such a church while their children leave and find their excitement elsewhere.

Parents must realize that their first responsibility before God is to their family. If the church has become more important than the relationships within your family, it is time to do some soul-searching and ask God to help you set your priorities in order. There is no question that leaving a church one has been part of for many years is hard. There will be those who do not understand and who will criticize your decision. There will be those who will turn away, and friendships may be lost. But there will also be those who understand and may even wish they had done the same thing before it was too late for their own children.

Leaving the church may not be necessary if you can encourage your child to become part of another church's youth group. You may be able to teach loyalty and commitment to your child by staying, while exercising positive alternative opportunities at the same time.

Tim LaHaye, in his book *The Family That Makes It,* gives five suggestions for choosing a family church. First, pray for wisdom, including the entire family in this prayer, even the rebellious teen. Good human judgment is important in making a choice, but only God knows what a church may become five years or more down the road. Second, loyalty to scriptural truth is primary. Does this church preach the Bible with passion and accuracy? Third, does this church minister to the entire family? Is good programming in place for all ages? Fourth, the church should provide each member of the family a place to serve God and find and use their spiritual gifts. Finally, would you confidently recommend this church to others? Would you invite your unchurched friends and acquaintances to visit?

A Bible-teaching church with a life-related message can make it considerably easier for parents to raise their children in the fear and admonition of the Lord.

Moving to a new church may not solve all the problems with your teenager. If he has not reached a stage where Mom and Dad feel threatened about making *any* request, they should insist he go with them to services. If it has always been understood that the family attends church together, this will not be surprising to him. Unfortunately, parents sometimes fold when their child begins to resist and becomes uncooperative about attending church. The misconception is that by making him attend church they will turn him off to God and the church, making him antagonistic to their beliefs. The truth is, he is already antagonistic and is asserting his right to make his own choices. Let him know you appreciate his cooperation in attending with the family, and you expect it will continue as long as he is living in your home.

Requiring a child to attend services isn't what turns him against the church. It is often the hypocrisy he sees there or in his home that makes the church a shallow mockery. We need to make our children aware that no church is perfect. We will always be able to find something wrong, something to criticize or be upset with. But in spite of imperfections, church is a place to have fellowship and group worship experiences that can be important to our spiritual growth.

It may also be true that your teen's growing interest in unacceptable activities may make him uncomfortable or cause him to rail against the "unreasonable" rules for behavior the church teaches. Let him be uncomfortable for an hour on Sunday morning. At least he is hearing an opposing view to what he is thinking. And if the view has some reasonableness attached to it, it may lodge somewhere and cause him to reconsider the choices he is making.

We should be careful not to give our children the impression that church attendance is what makes a person a Christian, or that he cannot find God anywhere except in the church. The institutional church can have real value for us as individuals and as a family, but God transcends the church as an organization. If our young people fall into the error of equating God with the imperfect church, they will have plenty to confirm their rebellious attitudes.

If parents do not make a serious attempt to keep their teenagers involved in youth meetings and social activities within the church, these teens will soon drift and make friendships that take them even further from the church. Boyfriends, girlfriends, and peer associations all pull hard to entangle our teen in activities that make Christian parents feel uneasy. It is better to insist they be part of youth activities in the church and encourage them to bring their friends—at least until it is obvious that their rebellion is uncontrollable.

God has created within us a need to socialize. We want to be loved, sought out, and included in whatever is going on. The church has the potential for being one of the finest sources of social contact available. Too often, however, selfishness and impersonal attitudes permeate even the life of the church.

Everyone, not just parents of teenagers, is concerned about the problems facing young people today: alcohol, drugs, promiscuous behavior, and rebellious attitudes; but far too few people are willing to do much about it. In the church, most recognize that a dynamic youth ministry is important, but too few want to be on the youth staff. Too many parents don't want to open their homes for social activities. Youth pastors often burn out after a few years of intense activity and too little help.

There seems to be a notion that working with teenagers takes a special gift, an unusual talent, or extensive training. Not so! The primary requirement for someone to work with young people is to love them. If a teenager senses your genuine concern for him as a person, he will respond to you. Nonjudgmental, unconditional love will go a long way toward drawing teenagers into a circle of friendship within the church.

What Can Parents Do?

You know your teenager needs more good, clean, wholesome activities to keep him busy and to help him grow socially. You know your church is lacking in some important areas, but there may be no other church in your community that can offer more. You are concerned about the interest your teen is developing in questionable activities. You know the time is coming when he will no longer accept your wishes about involvement in these things. So what steps should you take?

1. Go to your pastor and tell him your concerns about the need for more activities for young people in your church. Based on the responses you receive from him, be prepared to get actively involved in a parent group to promote more social opportunities for your teenagers.
2. If you have a youth pastor, talk with him and ask for suggestions as to how you can help him in this important area. Be careful not to imply criticism of his youth programming. Let him know you understand the limitation of his time and energy and you want to help. Offer to gather with a group of parents who will get teenagers together to plan some activities themselves with a little adult input and cooperation. If your youth pastor is married and has young children, offer to baby-sit so he and his wife can participate together without having to spend their meager salary on baby-sitters.
3. Get involved. If a bigger and better social life has the potential for drawing your teen back into the fellowship of the church, do not spare any effort to help.

Prayer

Father God, help me to open my heart and my home to the friends of my teenager. Give me ideas and energy to find ways to keep my teenager occupied in good, wholesome activities. Give me wisdom to discern the potentially dangerous and damaging influences on my child and help me to be strong in standing for what I believe is right. Amen.

Teens and the Unnatural High 8

We are a nation of drug users. A majority of Americans begin the day with a strong dose of caffeine to get them rolling. A large segment of our society depends on nicotine to help them move smoothly through the day. Over-tense mothers swallow anxiety-addressing pills to keep from yelling at the kids all day. We grab a Red Bull to give us energy to finish tasks when we are running out of steam. A growing segment of the population finds they need mood stabilizers to face the stresses of daily life. We finish off the day with a steaming cup of herbal tea, convinced that at last we have found the "pure" way to give us the much-needed bedtime calm. Others use alcohol to achieve many of the aforementioned effects.

Small wonder that our youth would follow in our footsteps! In an informal survey I did among high school youth in several evangelical churches, I learned that just about every teenager, ages thirteen to eighteen, knew where they could get almost any illicit drug within minutes or hours. Most denied ever trying these drugs, except alcohol. Most said whatever drug education they had received in school (if they remembered having had such a class) was inadequate. Surprisingly, a similar survey done twenty-five years ago revealed a more heavily drugged-up teen culture. In that survey, many were occasional marijuana users, had experimented with other illegal drugs, and often drank alcohol. These were teenagers also regularly involved in their church youth activities. Why have things improved over the last twenty-five years? It's hard to say. Maybe drug education *is* having more of an effect than even the teens know. Regardless, be sure your teenager is educated about the dangers of alcohol and other illegal drug use. Don't rely on someone else to give them information. Even if the situation is slightly better than it was twenty-five years ago, the problem certainly hasn't gone away.

Our children are living in a chemically influenced society. We should not be surprised to learn that they have experimented with something. Neither should we be overly alarmed and start calling the nearest drug addiction center when we suspect that our teen's experimentation with drugs might be happening more often than we thought. But as parents, we do need to be concerned. *Using* drugs is a short step away from *abusing* drugs. The drug scene, even experimentally, is especially insidious for children, because their bodies are still growing and their brains are developing. During the teen years so many changes are happening—personalities are being formed, value systems are developing. They are learning how to relate to others and are setting a course for themselves, whether they realize it or not, that will influence their entire future. They need to be at their best, free from mind-numbing, potentially disastrous drug use of any kind.

Parents need to follow up on what their children are learning in school and impress upon them the wisdom of staying drug- and alcohol-free. For some reason many parents assume that while all the world is drinking, smoking pot, and experimenting with other drugs, their child would not do such a thing—even if he is showing signs of rebellion. Find out something about the friends your child is associating with. Is it rumored or reported that they are drinkers? Druggies? If your child is spending much of his time with the drinking or drug-using crowd, chances are he also is involved.

Teen Alcohol Use Is Alarming

The National Institute on Alcohol Abuse and Alcoholism reported in 2005 that by the twelfth grade, three-fourths of children have consumed some alcohol. About two of every five eighth graders have tried alcohol at one time or another. What's worse, data shows that 11 percent of eighth graders, 22 percent of tenth graders, and 29 percent of twelfth graders have engaged in heavy binge drinking within the past two weeks. Also, research shows that adolescents are starting to drink at younger ages. In 2005, the average age of first use of alcohol was about fourteen. Information from 1965 showed the age then be around seventeen. Research also shows that the younger the adolescent is when he has that first drink the more likely he will continue to engage in behaviors that are harmful to him and to others.

Alcohol continues to be the drug of choice for adolescents. It is relatively inexpensive and easy to obtain, and many kids can get it directly from their own refrigerators or parents' liquor supply. Drinking among adolescents is widespread over all socioeconomic planes. It's not just boys who have been encouraged by well-meaning adults initiating them into adulthood with their first "buzz." It's girls, too. And sometimes the girls are supplying the alcohol.

Coupled closely with drinking patterns among adolescents are terrifying statistics relating to drinking and driving. According to a recent survey conducted by the National Highway Traffic Safety Administration, about 6.4 percent of 194.3 million drivers licensed in the United States are between the ages of sixteen and twenty. But this relatively small percentage of drivers is responsible for around 12 percent of all fatal crashes. According to the Century Council, four people under the age of twenty-one die each day in alcohol-impaired driving crashes.

Another frightening statistic is the rise in suicide rates among teenagers related to the depressant quality of alcohol. Physical fights, criminal acts, homicides, falls, and toxic poisoning are additional concerns for the alcohol-imbibing youth. Date rape, dating violence, and assaults are also often tied to drinking. Alcohol and teenagers are a bad combination.

From Use to Abuse

Since alcohol is the most used drug among teenagers, it's important for the parent to be knowledgeable in this area. Actual alcoholism is hard to define in teenagers. Often it's hard to detect a drinking problem in a teen until the problem is so serious that it causes extensive trouble in his life. The National Institute on Alcohol Abuse has defined a teenage problem drinker as a student who drinks moderate to heavy amounts of alcohol at least once a week, who gets roaring drunk about four times a year, and who gets into some kind of trouble as a result.

When does a teenager cross over the line and become a problem drinker? One working definition of alcoholism is that any alcohol use that impairs a person's health, social functioning, or societal adjustment is a problem for *that* drinker.

It is conceivable that a teenager could meet all of these criteria, other than "getting into trouble," and not be detected as having a drinking problem. It is also possible that a teenager could meet all of these criteria without anyone considering alcohol as the source of his trouble.

Some parents may not even have the foggiest notion that their children are drinking. They only notice little things that bother them. Or maybe the child is so adept at deception and concealment that the parent realizes nothing until the problem is full blown. Some parents know that their child is drinking, but are willing to leave him alone as long as he "handles" it. Some parents wonder, worry, and are afraid of what they suspect, but they feel utterly helpless to do anything about it.

Obtaining Other Drugs

Marijuana is the most commonly used illicit drug among teenagers in the United States. Use of this drug has decreased in the past decade, but according to the National Institute on Drug Abuse, prevalent rates of use have been fairly consistent over the past few years. Reports from the National Survey of Drug Use and Health (NSDUH, 2009) state that 11.8 percent of eighth graders, 26.7 percent of tenth graders, and 32.8 percent of twelfth graders have smoked marijuana in the previous year. Overall figures indicate that perhaps 21 percent of teenagers use marijuana fairly regularly.

While alcohol is the easiest drug to obtain, marijuana is also inexpensive and easy to come by. There are many reasons teens start using marijuana, probably the most prevalent one being curiosity. *Pot, Mary Jane, grass, reefer, skunk,* and *weed* are a few of the street names that have been romanticized in pop and rap songs, movies, and TV, giving kids the impression that it's cool to use it. Some adolescents find the calming effects of this drug a way to escape problems at home, at school, or with peers.

The risks of marijuana use include impaired short-term memory and problems with perception, judgment, and motor skills. Often the use of marijuana also involves alcohol. Frequent use of these drugs by immature and inexperienced youth can lead to dropping out of school—leaving them little chance of making it "out there" in the world.

Inquisitive teens can find a variety of illicit drugs to experiment with. There are stimulants, hallucinogens, inhalants, opioids, and prescription drugs. The parent who wants to be informed can go to the website of the National Institute on Drug Abuse to get the most current information on abused drugs and teen statistics.

Tobacco Addiction

One piece of good news is that cigarette smoking among teenagers is at its lowest point in the history of tobacco-use surveys. The bad news is the numbers are still much too high. A survey from the U.S. Centers for Disease Control and Prevention found that 50 percent of high school students have tried cigarette smoking at some point. Smoking rates are higher among teenagers than adults. Nationwide, about a quarter of high school students use some type of tobacco regularly, whether it's in the form of cigarettes, cigars, pipes, or smokeless (spit) tobacco. Girls are almost as likely to smoke as boys.

Addiction happens rapidly. Of all high school students who reported they smoked, three of every four had tried to quit, but failed. Many of them are still optimistic that they will quit eventually. The younger a child is when they smoke that first cigarette, the more likely it is that he will become a lifetime smoker. Recent surveys by the Centers for Disease Control indicate that about 10 percent of middle school students, eleven- to fourteen-year-olds, have used some form of tobacco in the past thirty days. These are frightening figures for parents.

What Can Parents Do?

There *are* things you can do as a parent, but first you must pay attention to what is going on with your child. Is your teen willing to talk about the dangers of alcohol and other drugs, or is he defensive? Does he seem moody beyond the expected behavior of adolescents? Is he excessively tired? Does he lack an appetite, or have a voracious one, constantly looking for goodies and carbohydrates? Take note of any behavioral changes that seem unusual for this child.

Also, know *where* your teenager is, *who he is with*, and *what they will be doing* while there. This is not so easy to do if your teenager is involved in secretive behavior and doesn't want to admit what he is doing when he's away from home. Check out his stories. Don't be snoopy, or accusatory. Just let him know that you are looking out for him, and you want to know what's going on in his life. And that you will check on his stories.

When committed to providing a home for your teen's friends to gather in, always be there when they gather. Don't be underfoot or constantly checking on what they're doing. Just let them know "you're around." Keep things under control. Ask other parents to do the same thing when your teen is invited to their homes.

Keep Communication Open

Talk straight with your teenager. Let him know that you understand he could find himself in a situation where there is drinking or drug use and things are getting out of hand. Get him to promise that he will call you to come get him, especially if he has had anything to drink. It is a fact that the one who is drinking is seldom aware of his impairments for driving, thus the horrible statistics relating to alcohol injuries and deaths. Let him know there will be no recriminations for this incident. (There might be a lot of discussion, though!) Your concern is for his safety and the safety of others that might be involved.

If your teen comes home intoxicated, don't try to preach to him or punish him while he is drunk—he won't remember and he won't care. Wait until he is sober and discuss, as calmly as you can, how important it is that he understands the dangers of alcohol and drugs. Teach. Don't merely punish.

But don't wait until the teen years. Talk to your children about alcohol and drugs as they are growing up. Have family discussions. Allow the children to speak what they think. It is your opportunity to hear their minds and bend them in a better direction. It is important that communication is open, and that family problems are shared if one member is having difficulties with alcohol or drugs.

What to Do When You Suspect Your Child Has a Problem

When a parent has sufficient reason to believe their child is drinking and the problem is serious, or could become serious, there are things he or she can do. If the child is at all willing to discuss his drinking with his parents, he may be willing to go through a simple questionnaire. The answers can help parent and child realize the extent of the problem.

Is My Drinking a Problem?[1]

1. Have I ever skipped school or left school because of drinking?

1. Adapted from James Comer and Alcoholics Anonymous.

2. Do I drink to make myself feel more at ease with my friends?
3. Do people call me a drinker? Or joke with me about using drugs?
4. If someone tells me I'm drinking too much, does it bother me?
5. Do I drink to escape worries or avoid doing things I should do?
6. Do I feel the need to drink before going out with my friends?
7. Do I seek others to buy booze for me?
8. Do I spend too much money on alcohol or drugs?
9. Has my drinking caused me to lose some of my old friends?
10. Do I hang out with the kids I am with now because they make it easy to get alcohol?
11. Do my friends drink less than I do?
12. Do I quickly empty my bottle, my can, or my glass and look for more?
13. Have I ever gotten in trouble driving because of alcohol or other drugs?
14. Do I get irritated when others talk to me about drinking, whether one-on-one or in a class lecture?
15. Have I ever had a loss of memory when I drink?
16. Do *I* think I might have a problem with booze?

A YES answer to even one of these questions is a warning. More than one yes answer may indicate that alcohol, or perhaps other drugs, have almost certainly become or are becoming a serious problem in a young person's life.

Do not underestimate the severity of the problem of drinking in your teenager. If you have concerns because of the answers your teenager has given, or if he has been unwilling to answer the questions, talk with someone who is knowledgeable about alcohol and its effects on teenagers. Go to your local alcohol treatment center and ask for printed information. Seek out a treatment counselor in the private sector, and be willing to pay for an hour to get information and potential help for your child. If your teenager is willing, take him with you.

Keep in mind you are not labeling your teenager an alcoholic. You are taking an aggressive stand to determine if alcohol use is becoming a problem in his life. Alcohol use by minors is illegal in most of the United States, so even if he's not drinking excessively, he is breaking the law. If your child is already having difficulties in school or with the family, you may be able to pinpoint the source of his real trouble—abuse of alcohol.

Questions Parents Should Ask Themselves

If you have questioned your child, and he is vehemently opposed to having any discussion with you about his drinking or drug use, ask yourself the following questions:[2]

1. Could I have answered YES for my teen for any of the questions on the "Is My Drinking a Problem?" survey?
2. If we parents have any alcohol in the house, have we noticed anything missing or diminished in *quality* (teens often drink from the parent stash and refill with water or another liquid)?
3. Does my child seem like a different person than the one I have known?
4. Can I count on my child to do what he is asked and take on responsibilities?
5. Does my child seem less interested in the things he used to enjoy?
6. Are his grades slipping? Is homework not being done? Are there concerned reports from teachers?

2. Adapted from "Twenty Questions for Parents" in Tom Alibrandi, *Young Alcoholics* (Minneapolis: CompCare Publications, 1978).

7. Have your child's friendships changed? Do you know who your child is hanging out with?
8. Have neighbors, friends, or others commented to you about your child's drinking?
9. Has your child been in any kind of trouble with the law?
10. Does your child defend his right to drink? ("All my friends do it.")
11. Does your child appear to "absent" himself from any conversations about alcohol?
12. Does your child get into fights with other teenagers?
13. Are you concerned about any medical or emotional problems or instabilities?
14. Do you feel OK about your teen's driving habits?
15. Is your teenager dishonest, or does she outright lie, about her activities?
16. If you drink, or you have adults around who do, does your child suddenly get helpful and volunteer to clean up after your social event (drinking his way through the leftovers)?
17. Do you find signs of drinking when doing a thorough housecleaning, or cleaning your child's room?
18. Do you ever detect the smell of alcohol on your child?
19. Does your child spend a lot of time alone, behind closed doors?
20. Are relationships within the family deteriorating around this child?

Any YES answers might be cause for concern, but if you realize there are a lot more yes answers than you thought there would be, seek help. Seek information. Confront your teenager with your concerns that he might be more affected by his alcohol use, and maybe other drug use, than he thinks. Maybe he will agree. It is more likely he will deny there are any problems or that he is drinking at all. You, the parents, will have to be this child's source of strength and his limit-setter. As the parents, you will have to do whatever it takes to get him to someone who can evaluate him and determine if he needs treatment.

What Parents Should NOT Do

If your child refuses to cooperate or gets angry and confrontational, pay attention to these DON'Ts:[3]

1. Don't confront your teen when he has obviously been drinking or appears "high."
2. Don't cover for your child or excuse his behavior.
3. Don't assume you can change your child's drinking behavior yourself. It may take the help of a professional who is trained in evaluating the extent of the problem and in addressing it. And, your child will have to cooperate in some measure.
4. Don't accept irrational, destructive behavior in the home. Do whatever needs to be done to gain control of the situation, including calling the authorities.
5. Don't nag, preach, or yell at the adolescent about his drinking. It will only make *you* upset.
6. Don't clean up after your drinking or drugging teenager. Let him experience the consequences of his behavior.
7. Don't allow yourself to be drawn into immature behavior because of your child's behavior.
8. Don't assume your child is just weak and has no willpower. He may be incapable of holding it together right now. He is in trouble and needs help to recover.

3. Adapted from Tom Alibrandi, *Young Alcoholics.*

9. Don't believe your child when he hurls "I hate you" at you when under the influence of his choices. It's not a question of loving or not loving. He may hate himself. Your reminders of his immature and dangerous behavior will only affirm his lack of self-worth.
10. Don't denounce your child with character-slamming words. Instead, express your anger at the crazy behavior and the alcohol or drugs that are behind it.
11. Don't let him get by with ignoring the rules you have set for the household. Set consequences and apply them as best you can. Force compliance if you can. Give him opportunities to show an effort. Expect him to succeed, but realize he may not be able to as long as alcohol is in the picture.
12. Don't follow him everywhere he goes. Parental watchdogging in this manner rarely works in the way hoped. It won't solve the problem and may make matters worse.
13. Don't give this child any money, except for vital necessities. Pay attention to how he spends the money you give him.
14. Don't make threats or warnings you are not prepared to follow through with. Act.
15. Don't give up. You are your child's most likely source of help.

When Your Child Wants Help With a Drinking Problem

If your teenager is willing to see a counselor or go along with treatment, one of the first things to do is to have a doctor give him a physical exam. The doctor should understand the problems of alcoholism and your concerns, and not only give a thorough physical examination but also impart medical information about alcohol. The doctor may suggest some form of medication that he thinks would be helpful. But make sure you ask questions about the medication. You don't want to exchange one form of addiction for another.

It can be a long, hard road back for the child who has a heavy dependency on alcohol. Remember, there is a strong probability that there is multi-drug use—not just alcohol. The child will need sustainers, comforters, and encouragers. The family will not be enough, but it must be the foundation.

Seek information about an Alcoholics Anonymous (AA) group that is made up of young persons. Maybe the local AA would be willing to sponsor a special group for teenagers. Consider an Al-Anon group for the family. If there is a Narcotics Anonymous organization in your community, talk with an organizer and see if this group might be appropriate for a multi-drug user in recovery.

Perhaps this child needs in-patient treatment. He may need to detoxify under careful supervision and get away from the "old crowd" for a period of time. It might be important for him to receive a power-packed education about alcohol and gain some tools to use when he returns to former temptations. It will take time for him to think about himself more clearly.

There will be emotional ups and downs for the family that has a teenage problem drinker. The whole family suffers and can become sick itself, in a different way but one that is as potentially destructive. It is vital that the problem be recognized and dealt with as early as possible, before it permeates through the family. Mom and Dad and perhaps siblings will need supportive friends and extended family. Keeping the family strong and stable will provide a healing foundation for this child.

Other Drugs Are Harder to Detect

The use or abuse of other drugs may not be as easy to detect as alcohol. As was stated earlier, for teenagers, other drug use often accompanies alcohol use. You can use the same questions cited in this chapter to lead you to similar conclusions about other drugs. Especially with marijuana, it is not too difficult for the user to hide his intoxicated condition. It's usually pretty obvious when someone is drunk on alcohol, but a person who is high on pot has the ability to hide his high, to "come down," and carry on a seemingly normal conversation.

Often a parent's first realization that their child may be involved in drug use comes when they discover pills or paraphernalia tucked away in a drawer or other hiding spot. There may be remnants of marijuana in the form of tiny seeds or funny-looking leaf fragments. Often the puzzled parent wonders what this stuff is without considering that their child might be using illicit drugs.

Parents who know their child well have an almost uncanny sense that something is wrong in their child's demeanor or behavior. Some parents, however, don't know their child well enough to be aware of subtle changes, or they attribute these changes to other things—normal, expected adolescent behavior or problems with school or friends. Sometimes they suspect there may be a problem but just don't want to deal with it. Other things may be going on in the lives of the parents that distract them or drain them emotionally. It is important to understand that your teen's drinking or drug use won't go away by itself. In spite of whatever else may be going on, parents must take action to help their child.

Recognizing Illicit Drug Use in Your Teenager

Following is a list of possible behavioral changes that occur in kids who are involved in drug use. Be alert to any of these in your child:

- poor attendance at school or multiple late notices
- changes in grades or work habits
- a lack of concern about personal hygiene and appearance
- a tendency to argue or fight
- a tendency to be secretive about peer associations
- a decrease in the ability to concentrate
- lethargic behavior

- wears sunglasses more often (to hide dilated or constricted pupils)
- a declining appetite
- a tendency to keep arms covered (to cover possible track marks, or self-mutilation)
- an increase in euphoria or disproportionate excitement
- problems with coordination—staggering or stumbling
- trouble staying awake when not engaged in physical activity
- inflamed nose and eyelids
- allergy-like symptoms
- prolonged sleeplessness
- a tendency to be suspicious of others
- an inability to notice pain
- inattentiveness, staring, or difficulty remembering simple things
- jerky eye movements, facial grimaces, tics
- slow, slurred speech, jerking muscles, bizarre behaviors
- a depressed mood

This list is not exhaustive, and obviously any number of physical illnesses and ailments can cause some of these same reactions in your child, but when they occur with a degree of regularity, or when there seems to be no basis for this kind of behavioral change, suspect drug experimentation or use.

Be Informed

Find out about drug abuse in your community. Talk to other parents. Talk to your child's counselor at school. Talk to other kids. Invite other parents to meet with you to talk about the potential problems for your community youth. Make it clear the purpose is not to find fault or accuse, but to help each other know what is going on and seek a positive approach to helping your children. Talk with the youth leaders in your church. Ask them what they know about the alcohol and drug use in the teenagers they work with. Maybe they are young and a little naïve, and would welcome wise adult input.

Educate yourself about the effects of drugs, especially the drugs that are being used and abused in your community. Engage your children and their friends in casual conversation. Talk about what you are learning and ask them what they think. Take a firm and clear stand against drug use. Have rules that make sense, and enforce them. Be sure your teenager knows what is expected and what the punishment will be if he ignores the rules. Talk with the parents of your child's friends regularly. Back each other up. Encourage each other. Work together to plan fun, meaningful, constructive alternatives for your children that will keep them busy and involved apart from the drug and alcohol scene.

Remember that your child's first experience with alcohol or other drugs will not come from scary-looking pushers or dealers. They will likely receive their first drugs from friends or kids they hang out with. It will seem like an adventure in the beginning, a shared non-parent-approved thing. Recognize that your teenager will fight to maintain his circle of friends, no matter what unacceptable things they may be doing. You, the parent, must hang in there, fighting for your child's welfare. You must be willing for your child to hate you for a while, while you are showing him consistent love, strong love, tough love.

It is hard to be an adolescent in today's world. There are few places to find responsible ways to contribute to the world he lives in. Jobs are scarce or unavailable until one is experienced or old enough. The teenager is becoming physically and emotionally capable of being part of the adult world, but he is told, "Not yet." What is he to do in the meantime? For some, alcohol and drugs seem to fill the void. As a responsible parent, do what you need to do in order to ensure that your teenager will not be sidetracked in life by immature choices and addictions that will rob him of a future.

May God be your strength and give you the courage to do what you must.

Something to Do

1. Your child may not be involved with alcohol or drugs. Read this chapter with him and tell him of your concerns about the teenage world he lives in every day. Ask him to commit to you that he will not allow himself to be tempted, no matter what his friends say or do. Let him know he can talk to you about the temptations, and you can, together, seek answers to his questions. If he has friends he is worried about, talk about what he might be able to do to help them. Be willing to help him if he asks you.
2. If you suspect your child might be using alcohol or drugs, tell him you've been reading a book to help you understand a little more about the teenage world he lives in. Ask him to read this chapter with you, because you want to know what he's thinking about these things and how he is affected by them with his friends. This is not to expose him, or accuse him, but to give him an opportunity to talk about this aspect of his life in a calm, rational way.
3. If you are aware that your child is using and/or abusing alcohol or drugs of any kind, follow the suggestions in this chapter and don't delay in seeking help.

Prayer

God, protect my child. I know there is an enemy bent on destroying him and our family. Help me to know, or discover, what my child may be doing that could be harmful to him, and give me the wisdom and the strength to confront it and rescue him from potential danger. Amen.

The Lure of Sex 9

"I can't stand to look at her! How could she do this?" These words came from a grief-stricken mother who had just learned that her fourteen-year-old daughter had spent most of the night with several boys—older than she—in the home of one of the boys while his parents were out of town. The mother was assuming the worst. The daughter was admitting nothing. She wasn't even speaking to her parents.

Did she? Or didn't she? What would *you* assume about your daughter or son given a similar set of circumstances and the daily influences that surround their lives?

This Christian mother was immediately ready to assume the worst about her daughter. Her next thought was to get her to the family planning clinic and get her on the pill—all natural reactions based on shock, hurt, and disappointment.

How should parents face the growing tide of sexual activity among our youth?

Facts Parents Need to Know

According to data from the Centers for Disease Control and Prevention, almost 25 percent of all females, and 30 percent of all males have had some premarital sexual experience by the time they reach the age of fifteen. That number increases to 66 percent of females and 68 percent of males by the age of eighteen. That number is down from data received in the '90s, but it is still alarming to consider that premarital intercourse is a relative norm for males and females over the age of eighteen, as shown in the same study.

What about younger teens? Teens themselves report that the age of sexual initiation is getting younger. One high school senior reported, "I'd say that about half the girls in my graduating class are virgins, but you wouldn't believe those freshman and sophomore girls. By the time *they* graduate, there won't be any virgins left!" That may be a more dire thought than data shows, but considering the many influences that surround our youth today, it is frightening to consider what pressures our young men and women are daily facing in their social world.

Premarital sexual behavior, particularly the act of intercourse, has become more acceptable for teens of all ages than it was for previous generations. While our grandparents sometimes engaged in premarital sex, they didn't talk about it or promote it. "Good girls" didn't do "it." Or at least they didn't tell others they did. Today's teens are not reluctant to share their experiences with one another and even encourage one another to lose their virginity.

Other acts that are not seen as particularly "sexual" or compromising—including oral sex, mutual masturbation, and what used to be called "dry humping"—are often considered "safe sex." "If I do those things, I'm still a virgin, right?" is a frequent question asked by young teens in an ABC poll.

Today's teenagers are not so different from yesterday's teenagers. Curiosity about the opposite sex and sexual acts have always been part of the "coming of age" process.

Some of the things that may be different for our teens today include an earlier onset of puberty; relative freedom from parental restraints; cues from a pleasure-bent, sex-saturated society; and ready access to birth control measures—whether they use them or not.

One study from the U.S. Department of Health and Human Services states that many girls have their first sexual experience in their own homes, or perhaps the home of their male partner, near the age of fifteen. Summer appears to be the season of first experiences—when temptation and opportunity peak together.

Why do girls, who seem to have the most to lose, get involved in sexual experimentation? Reasons girls give often reflect their desire to please. "I just couldn't say no. He would be disappointed." "I wanted him to be happy with me." "I wanted him to like me more." "I wanted to make him feel good." "He expected it from me." Other reasons girls gave were: wanting to be close, to be held, and to feel cared about. They wanted to have a special relationship with someone who truly liked them. They felt alone and needed someone to belong to.

Guy's reasons were more often centered on personal satisfaction and pleasure. "I felt sexy, and I wanted to have some fun." "I wanted my girlfriend to know I was a man, and show her how much of a man I was." "I couldn't stop. We had gone too far." "She led me on, and then, well, we just did it." "I was drinking and didn't know what I was doing."

These are comments I have heard in my counseling office, and they are similar to what is found in studies cited through other sources. One additional comment heard more often now, is: "It's what you do when you have a special boyfriend/girlfriend." In other words, it's become a "natural" part of a steady relationship.

Reasons given for not getting involved sexually include: "I didn't know him/her well enough . . . yet." Or "There was no place private to go."

Two of the most powerful predictors of whether a guy or girl will be sexually active are how many of their same-sex peers they believe are sexually active and how widely accepted they believe their sexual activity will be. So if your teenager is part of a group of kids who feel themselves to be sexually "liberated," chances are your teen may be feeling the same way.

On the other hand, teenagers who refrain from sexual activity believe their peer group is supportive of their abstinence. This is usually most true among teens that are part of a religious body. Exceptions often arise when an exclusive boyfriend-girlfriend relationship develops, and time and togetherness creates an intimacy that moves toward physical expression.

Our children are growing up in a society that encourages sexual activity without marriage. It is irrational for parents to think their teens can't be affected by this—or to be shocked when they are. It is even more irrational to condemn them for their immaturity and for surrendering to their natural inclinations.

Teens Are Besieged With Sexual Messages

A study done several years ago showed that more than 80 percent of the top twenty TV shows among teenage viewers contained some sexual content, including 20 percent with sexual intercourse. Almost half of the top secular CDs contained sexual content, with nearly 20 percent including explicit descriptions of sexual intercourse. Music videos contained close to ninety-five sexual situations per hour, including hard core sex scenes such as intercourse and oral sex. We need to be aware of what our children are watching and listening to. We need to talk to them about what they are bombarded with—and restrict its availability in their lives.

The Internet is a hotbed of sexuality. Online pornography is easy to access. Our children can accidentally, or purposefully, find anything sexual with just the click of the mouse. And once they access it, it is very difficult to disengage.

The Parent Sex Talk

For most parents, their children arrive at sexual maturity almost without warning. One day we have a child. The next, it seems, we have an attractive, perhaps voluptuous, daughter, who is delighted with the male attention she is receiving. And the little boy who was playing with trucks in the sand is overnight a lusty young male on the prowl. Suddenly the sex education we were planning to give them "when the time was right" is way past due, and there seems to be no comfortable way to approach the subject.

Parents have never been good at discussing sex with their children. Even in the "enlightened" and easy-talking age we live in, a study done by *Time,* Health & Science (SearchTime.com) indicates that more than 40 percent of sexually active adolescents had intercourse before their parents talked to them about sex. According to an ABC News poll, about 90 percent of parents nationwide said they have talked to their teens about sex. However, only half of their teens agreed they had been given "the talk." So whatever parents think the sex talk is, it isn't being "caught" by their teenagers.

The irony is, polls indicate that most teenagers do want to learn about sex from their parents. Do parents not consider themselves good enough teachers or do they think they aren't knowledgeable enough? Or is it because there is some shyness about bringing the subject of sex and sexual activity up with our children? Maybe so. And perhaps it is also because we, as parents, are still not comfortable with our own sexuality or our own experience, either in marriage or out of it, and thus we find it difficult to discuss this subject with clarity and conviction. Whatever the reasons, our children are the losers in this "battle for the body." Parents are not doing their job. They are sometimes fearful of what their children may be taught by others—afraid they lack control over the information presented to their children—but if they don't personally try to educate their children about sex, they have no one to blame but themselves.

Many parents want more than a list of how-to's and how-not-to's for their children. They are against any kind of sex education that doesn't teach healthy attitudes and morals at the same time. But the church is often reluctant to enter wholeheartedly into the area of sex education. The church is the parents' greatest ally against the decadent moral culture our children are growing up in, but we are deceiving ourselves if we think all our children need to hear is "No" and "Don't do it."

Many parents accept the biblical standard that sex outside of the marriage relationship is wrong. Wise ones know that the scriptural admonition to "flee youthful lusts" (2 Timothy 2:22 KJV) has many reasons behind it—not just to deny youthful pleasure for discipline's sake. One of these reasons has to do with the possible product of sexual intercourse.

Teen Pregnancy

Pregnancy is perhaps the first problem we think of when we consider teenagers and sex. Youth who are committed to sexual activity either with a single partner or promiscuously very often take care of themselves and will use some form of contraception. However, they often lack the knowledge and experience to use it correctly. It is frightening how little they really understand about the reproductive process and how to prevent conception.

One common belief among teenagers is: "You can't get pregnant if he lets go outside of you." Obviously, this method of contraception takes no account of pre-ejaculatory sperm and also expects a great deal of control from a teenage male. Another belief is: "You can't get pregnant if you have sex standing up." Again, there's a lack of knowledge about the capacity of sperm to reach its target by swimming "upstream." The rhythm method is not judged to be especially reliable even in marriage, but is considered safe by many teenage girls. What is most overwhelming is the number of girls who believe their "safe" time is the middle week between periods—the exact time when conception is most likely. Also, many of these girls' menstrual cycles are still developing and are not regular, making any kind of rhythm method unreliable under the best of circumstances.

Boys, if they are concerned about taking responsibility for contraception, sometimes use substitutes for condoms that might be humorous if the possible consequences were not so serious. Young males who are too shy about purchasing the right equipment, or don't want to appear prepared to take advantage of their girlfriend, might use sandwich bags, plastic wrap, or anything else they think might contain the fluid. Effective? Only if very lucky.

For many other teenagers whose first and perhaps continued experiences with sexual intercourse are spontaneous and impulsive, virtually no attempt is made to prevent pregnancy. Young persons who allow their innocent kissing to turn into passionate desire very often find themselves at a point of no return. Without pre-planning and predetermined standards of sexual behavior, too many girls find they have teased themselves into a situation where there is no backing up. Too many young men find they have crossed over the line and they no longer have any desire to control their lust. Passion has taken over. They virtually cannot stop themselves, and if the girl is as out-of-control as the guy, intercourse will happen. Often this is followed by fear, guilt, remorse, and shame.

Then what? Statistics tell us that pregnancy usually happens within the first six months of a relationship if the couple is sexually active. The Guttmacher Institute study on teens and sexual behavior reports that approximately three in ten young women ages fifteen to nineteen in the U.S. become pregnant at least once before they reach the age of twenty. When you add girls ages fourteen and under, that number could increase to four in ten (American Academy of Pediatrics).

The chances of your daughter becoming pregnant, then, may be three or four in ten. The chances of your son fathering a child during his teen years are about the same—maybe higher if he is promiscuous in his relationships with girls.

A Not-So-Untypical Story

Many years ago, I was the area representative for a national Christian adoption agency. One young couple I worked with is a good example of what can happen in a teenager's world. She was seventeen, a professing Christian, active in her small church's youth group. He was fifteen, good-looking, athletic, charming, and interested in her. He was not involved in church. She, flattered that he was interested in her, invited him to her youth group. He came several times, but was interested in her, not the youth group. They dated for a while, spent a lot of time together at her home and his, and eventually he charmed her into having sex with him. She was remorseful and broke up with him. He pursued her and she succumbed again. Within several months she was pregnant. Now they were seeing me, at the demand of her parents, to give this baby up for adoption. That wasn't my role, but it was my responsibility to give them all the information they needed if they were to keep this baby and raise it themselves.

He was fifteen and not interested in marriage. She was a senior in high school, the baby due around graduation time. Her parents refused to accept the baby into their lives, so if she kept the baby, she would be on her own. She seemed to have no choice.

Then, during her pregnancy, she discovered that he had already fathered another child with a girl who was a junior in the same high school. The other girl's baby was born. She kept the child—and brought it to school to show everyone, letting them know who the father was. My young client was devastated. The fifteen-year-old father begged her to forgive him, explaining it was a mistake and that he only wanted to be with her.

When the baby was born, the girl with great grief gave the baby into the arms of the adopting mother. Shortly thereafter she learned that while she was pregnant with his baby, he had impregnated another girl in her senior class whose baby would be born that next fall.

The great irony of this sad story is that in the state where this occurred, *she* could have been charged with statutory rape since she turned eighteen while they were still sexually active.

Options for Pregnant Teenage Girls

So what happens to a teenage girl who finds herself pregnant? Maybe she is in a similar situation to that of my young client, anticipating a lifetime of regret and sadness, wondering about the child she'll never know. Just a few decades ago, unwed mothers who kept their children were not socially acceptable. Their options were to marry the young man, if he were willing; to give birth and then give the baby to an adoptive family; to try to get an illegal abortion somewhere or attempt to abort the baby themselves; or to commit suicide.

Time has not changed a woman's options much, with two important exceptions. First, unwed mothers who keep their babies are now much more acceptable—even considered noble in some circles—and the state will give them financial assistance to take care of their children. Many women—teenagers as well as older women—are choosing to get pregnant outside of marriage. The cost can be great to a young mother who discovers it takes way more than love to raise a child, and to the older mother who realizes it is not so easy to be a single parent.

Abortion Is Legal

The second difference for today's young woman who finds herself unexpectedly pregnant is that she now has the option of terminating that pregnancy through legal abortion, without the knowledge or consent of her parents or guardians. And, without the consent of the boy who fathered the child.

Abortion is perhaps one of the hottest topics of debate both politically and morally. Many people, including most Christians, do not consider abortion an option at all. In pure and simple terms, abortion is seen as murder. It's the destruction of a human life at the whim of a more powerful human being. Sadly, in this case, the more powerful human is the one who gave life in the first place—the baby's mother. Roughly 30 percent of teenage pregnancies end in abortion.

There is no way to discuss the matter of abortion without great emotion. In her book *In Necessity and in Sorrow*, Dr. Magda Denes writes of life and death in an abortion hospital. She describes herself as a traitor to her own beliefs—she was in full support of the legality and necessity of abortion. But in her book she speaks of the horror of it. She herself went through the trauma of abortion.

Because of her own unexpected reactions to her decision to abort her third pregnancy, she felt the desire to search out the feelings and circumstances of others involved in abortions.

Her most basic conclusions revolve around the incomprehensible tragedies that embed humanity. She interviewed abortion patients, doctors and nurses who performed and attended abortions, and persons involved in the lives of abortion patients—parents, boyfriends, husbands. She viewed abortion techniques and aborted babies firsthand.

Her book is about stress, need, sorrow, isolation, fear, and aloneness beyond comprehension. It is a treatise on a subject we too often stand back from and withhold our opinions. Many of us have never been closely involved with the agonizing trauma of a young girl we love and would give our life for, who is pregnant.

The book was written in 1976, but the realities of the author's observations still hold true today. Even though our world has attempted to make abortion an accepted way of life, those who experience it still suffer.

Beliefs Challenged

There is dreadful sadness when parents who have expressed anger about legalized abortion find that their own teenage daughter is pregnant. Their vehement convictions may be assailed as they consider what giving birth to an infant means to their child's physical, mental, and emotional well-being, not to mention her future. They may suddenly find themselves wondering if it might not be the best solution after all. They then face the double agony of their daughter's pregnancy and their own double standard. There is no easy answer. From there they may be dismayed to learn they do not have a voice in preventing their young daughter from having an abortion. Nor can they force her to have one against her will.

But what about the young girl? There are those who would say, "She had her fun; let her pay for it." But was it fun? And *who* will pay for it? Not only will the girl pay, but also her parents, the baby, the young man who fathered the child, and even society. No, it's not only the problem of a single young girl. It's a problem we all share.

Mark Twain once said, "It is easy to bear adversity—*another* man's (*or woman's*), I mean" (words in italics in parentheses added). We find it easy to give pat answers when they do not involve our own well-being. An unwanted pregnancy changes a girl's life completely. No matter what option is chosen, there will never be a perfect ending. There are consequences that will affect the girl for the rest of her life. Parents need to be prepared to give their daughter all of the support they can during the difficult weeks of making her decision. They need to remind her that this tiny life growing within her is a real person—that in spite of the circumstances of her pregnancy, God has breathed life into this little one, and she must think about what it means to choose to snuff out that life. It is wise to find someone else you trust and respect to discuss with her the options of adoption or keeping the child—maybe a pastor, a family friend, or a professional counselor, who can help her understand the consequences of each choice she might make.

Once her decision is made, it is important to stand with her, whether you agree with her choice or not. You don't need to support an abortion, should she so choose, but you must be there for your daughter. There will be pain. There will be grief. There will be sorrow, if not now, in the future. Speak what you feel, express *your* sorrow, and remind your daughter you do understand how difficult this is for her. If she chooses abortion, you can express your disagreement with her choice, but continue to love her and be there for her.

A young married woman in her early thirties, with three children, came to my office. She was trying to settle an old wound in her life. She had had an abortion in her teen years. It had seemed the only thing to do. Her parents never knew of it. When she confessed this to her mother, after she was married and had borne her first child, her mother in "righteous anger" turned away from her, distancing herself from her daughter for seven years. The mother essentially cut herself off from the joy of her grandchildren and the mother-daughter relationship she could have experienced. God had forgiven her daughter. But she, self-righteously, would not. Eventually, with much prayer and counsel, the mother was able to accept and understand what her daughter had done, and they were restored. She had mistakenly believed that by shunning her daughter she was rightly defending her belief about the sin of the abortion. She had forgotten, however, that the Scripture also speaks of repentance and forgiveness and restoration. It was *my* joy to see this mother and daughter embracing one another tightly as they each yielded to God's whole truth.

Young Men Are Affected Too

If it is your son who has fathered a child, whatever he may want is beyond his control. The girl will make all the decisions, with or without his agreement or support. He will need to have someone to help him make responsible choices and someone to talk to about his frustrations and future choices. Maybe that person or persons will be his parents. Maybe it will be someone else. Don't suppose that he has no feelings or doesn't feel a sense of responsibility toward the girl and the baby. He may present a cold, stubborn attitude, or he may crumble. He needs his mom and dad.

If the girl chooses to have the baby and keep it, he can be made financially responsible for this child for eighteen years, and he may choose to be responsible for many years beyond that. This child will always be a part of his life to come. It will affect his future family, his future income, and possibly his future choice of education and occupation.

Attitudes About Contraception

What about contraceptive measures for sexually active teenagers? Maybe you suspect your child is having sexual relations. There may not be any proof, just a constant fear that because a relationship is developing, or because of the crowd your child runs with, it is a real possibility. Maybe you have been through the pregnancy scare and are now wondering what you can or should do. You may be thinking to yourself, *I don't believe in premarital sex. I don't want to encourage my child to be sexually involved with anyone. I don't want to show my lack of trust, or push my child into something they may not even be thinking about.*

Newsflash! If your teenager is normal, he or she *is* thinking about it. And parents must face the fact that if their child is moving into a rebellious lifestyle—away from parental values—the probability is strong that active sexuality will be a part of it. Parents who strongly believe in scriptural standards of sexuality for themselves and for their children will find it extremely difficult to deal with the subject of contraceptives for their teenager. But the matter must be faced.

Parents Must Face Their Own Standards of Sexuality

Parents must, first of all, sit down together and discuss their own personal attitudes and biases as rationally as possible. Maybe this would be a good time to talk about the subject with a qualified and trusted third party.

This is often a hard subject to talk about, whether with each other or with someone else, and especially with teenage children, but while parents are failing to *talk* about it, many of their children are *doing* it. It's time to step up and say what needs to be said and do what needs to be done.

Parents need to reaffirm their own standards to their children or *affirm* them if they have never spoken of them before. It's somewhat tricky for parents to do this without making insinuations to their teenager. The truth is, before we can speak comfortably to our children about these delicate matters, we need to feel at least somewhat comfortable about them ourselves. If Mom and Dad have a mature and realistic attitude about their own sexuality, chances are they will be able to communicate well with their children.

If not, honest and open communication may still be possible, as Mom and Dad become honest about their own sexual hang-ups. That kind of honesty might pry open the door of communication with their teenager.

Some parents cannot in good conscience before the Lord take their child to a family planning clinic to be educated about contraceptives, but they can sit down with their child and confess their discomfort in discussing sex and provide him with essential information by word or printed material that does not violate their own moral standards. There are numerous publications that promote morality while giving vital information to young people who desperately need it. At the end of this chapter, I've listed several excellent books for parents and teenagers. They are available online or at your local Christian bookstore.

Don't give anything to your child to read, however, that you, as the parent, have not read first. Be knowledgeable. Be in a position to discuss these things with intelligence and without biased misinformation.

The Reality of Sexually Transmitted Diseases

Pregnancy is not the only consequence for sexually active teens. Your child needs to know that any kind of sexual activity carries with it the possibility of contracting a sexually transmitted disease (STD). Startling research by the U.S. Centers for Disease Control found that at least one in four American teenage girls has a sexually transmitted disease. The most common, human papillomavirus (HPV), can cause cervical cancer, and the second most common, Chlamydia, carries with it the possibility of infertility. Infected girls might never be able to conceive a baby, even as happily married women anxious to begin their families.

Sexually active teenagers often consider themselves immune to any negative consequences of their behavior. The reality is each year there are approximately 10 million new STD infections among youth ages fifteen to twenty-four. In 2006, about 14 percent of all persons diagnosed with HIV/AIDS were ages thirteen to twenty-four, which adds up to more than 5,000 youth. Too many of our precious young people's lives may be ending before they even begin, or they may be setting themselves up for a lifetime of physical disability and pain.

Many STDs can be treated with various medications, but they have to be caught in order to be treated, and many teenagers are either woefully ignorant of symptoms or too embarrassed or afraid to tell anyone who might be able to help.

Whether or not you suspect your child is engaging in sexual behavior, give him the information. Even if he isn't sexually active, he can help friends who might confide in him. If you know your child is sexually active, and she knows you know, plead with her to have a physical examination, with no recriminations, just to be sure she is disease-free. And then plead with her to reconsider her behavior.

You cannot regulate or even always be knowledgeable about your child's sex life. You can keep what you consider a twenty-four-hour watch on your offspring and feel certain you are shielding your child from all sexual activity, and yet come up with a pregnant teenager or a son with a venereal disease. If sex is what they want, they will find a way in spite of you.

Abstinence Education

What about abstinence? If a girl, or a young man, chooses to wait until marriage to experience sex, there is no concern for unwanted pregnancies, guilt, or shame. No worries about sexually transmitted diseases. So then, what about abstinence education? How effective is it? Does it really change anything?

A study done by the National Campaign to Prevent Teen and Unplanned Pregnancy shows that a theory-based, well-designed program that focuses only on abstinence *can* help young adolescents delay becoming sexually active. Unfortunately, this kind of abstinence-only program does not meet the criteria for federal funding. The program used in the study contained accurate information and portrayed sex positively. It was not said to be simply "moralistic." But still it did not meet federal criteria.

There are those who think it is not possible to keep teenagers from having sex. They consider it a part of the growing-up experience. Be assured, there are still young people who are making the decision to wait until their wedding night to have their first sexual experience. Is it easy? No. People committed to that standard will certainly feel pressure to let go of their resolve. When they believe they are in love and that they've found their lifetime partner, they will be tempted to express their feelings sexually. But if they do, they are often disappointed and disillusioned as that "sure thing" blows up, and they find they have given themselves to the wrong person and can't take it back.

For some parents, the loss of their child's virginity (either male or female) seems to be the most unutterably terrible thing that could happen to their child. For many parents who deeply care about their child's relationship with God, virginity seems to take precedence over almost everything else. Parents need to come to an understanding that God does not categorize sins, but He does take special notice of the attitude of the heart in relation to the activities of the sinner. For the parent to attack the *actions* is to ignore the heart cry of the child who needs to be dealt with in a more thoughtful and caring way.

Parents Need to Stand Firm on Their Convictions

Parents do not have to compromise their own beliefs and convictions. In fact, they need to stand on them firmly and confirm them to their teens. Parents who vacillate in this area because of fear or an attempt not to appear "old-fashioned and out of touch" will lose their child's respect. According to many studies, most teenagers still feel that premarital sex is not right, but they engage in it anyway. When their mom and dad give an implied OK by not addressing the issue, it confuses them.

Give your child information and direction, not license for unrestricted sexual behavior. Let them know you are aware they will make their own decisions regarding their sexual choices. Your hope is that they will make those decisions thoughtfully, not under the pressure and excitement of "the moment."

Most important, let them know that their sexuality and sex drive are gifts from God to be used in the sacred commitment of marriage for a lifetime. Let them understand that the definition of adultery is sex outside of marriage. When they choose to have indiscriminate sex, they are committing adultery against their future life partner. And they will live to regret it.

That truth may not mean much to them in the lust of youth, but they need to receive the message anyway. It is important that they understand from early childhood that their body is private and to be shared only with the person they will one day marry. Ignorant references to sex, including inappropriate language, should not be countered by parents with shock, but with education and spiritual truth in words that even the youngest can comprehend.

Tell your children when they are old enough to understand that you are praying God will bring the most wonderful person into their lives at the right time, and you are praying that person will be just as pure and innocent as they are. Remind them of this often.

Also remind your teenagers that they will answer to God for decisions that are contrary to His standards. This is not necessarily God's punishment. It is the law of natural consequences. Be sure they know what the Bible says about their sexual behavior. Let them know what you want for them and hope for them—and that's why you come on a little strong sometimes. Let them know you will be disappointed if they make choices that deviate from your standards, which are biblical standards. But also let them know there are no circumstances that will be so awful that you, as their parent, will turn away from them. They need to know that while they may disappoint you or anger you, you will always love them and be there when they need you.

Restored Virginity

Our teenagers also need to have the reassurance that if they have lost their virginity, there is a case to be made for "restored virginity." Many years ago, I was privileged to attend an international youth conference where Josh McDowell—the main speaker at the event—gave the invitation to young men and women who had previously made the choice to have sex, to make a new choice. Hundreds of teenagers came to the altar, committing to live a restored life of virginity until marriage. Many of them probably failed to keep that commitment, but the intentions in their hearts revealed a desire in these youth to "do it God's way."

Jim Burns, founder of the ministry of HomeWord, writes[1] that a growing number of young people are committing themselves to the Purity Code. They are making a choice that goes against everything their youthful society is telling them:

> In honor of God, my family, and my future spouse, I commit my life to sexual purity. This involves:
>
> 1. Honoring God with my *body*
> 2. Renewing my *mind* for the good
> 3. Turning my *eyes* from worthless things
> 4. Guarding my *heart* above all else

You may think it is too late to challenge your teenager with this kind of thinking, especially if they are rebelling against going to church and don't want to talk about God. It's never too late to give your child information that might sink in and take root, eventually. They might not want to hear it from you, but they might read it, out of curiosity, if the book is left lying around. Maybe they have already violated that code, and wish they hadn't. Or maybe they are caught up in pornography or behaviors they don't know how to change. Don't preach or try to teach. Give them opportunity to hear another voice.

1. Jim Burns, *The Purity Code* (Minneapolis: Bethany House, 2008), 16.

Dating Violence and Rape

One other issue needs to be addressed: teen dating violence and rape. Not all girls, or guys for that matter, who lose their virginity lose it willingly. Several years ago the U.S. Department of Justice reported that females ages sixteen to twenty-four are more vulnerable to intimate partner violence than any other age group—a rate nearly triple the national average. An article in the *Journal of the American Medical Association* reported that approximately one in five female high school students reported being physically and/or sexually abused by a dating partner. Another resource says that 58 percent of rape victims are between the ages of twelve and twenty-four. Half of the reported date rapes occur among teenagers.

Meanwhile, 81 percent of parents surveyed in a 2004 *Woman's Health* article either did not believe teen dating violence was an issue or they admitted they had not thought of it as an issue.

Boys are vulnerable too, but they are far less likely to report incidences of rape or violence. Many young men fall victim to rape by another male, usually older. Young men can experience rape by a woman as well. The guilt they feel can be just as debilitating as that of a young woman who has lost her virginity in an act of abuse or violence. There are few reliable statistics related to young men being abused by young women in a dating relationship, partly because it is hard to admit to being victimized when you are a guy.

Parents Must Act

This may have been a hard chapter for many parents to read, but the truths stated here cannot be avoided. Your child needs you to be knowledgeable. Your child needs you to be available. Your child may need you to confront his or her out-of-control sexual behavior. Most important, your child needs you to love him or her in spite of what you might know or suspect.

So what happened to the fourteen-year-old at the beginning of this chapter? As it turns out, she did not have sex while she was hanging out with these boys. The boys might have been thinking about it, but they didn't act. She was mortified that her mother thought she had had sex. She grieved because her mother didn't trust her and thought her capable of doing such a thing. Her mom overreacted. But given the information put forth in this chapter, this young lady made a very unwise choice, and it could have turned out much differently. That said, as a parent it's important to stay calm and not jump to conclusions.

Parents, take the opportunity to give your children the much-needed information that will help keep them safe during these vulnerable years. It's never too late to do the right thing.

Something to Do

1. Buy or borrow one or all of the following books:

   What's Love Got to Do With It? (talking to your kids about sex) by John T. Chirban (Nashville: Thomas Nelson, 2007)

   Love, Sex, and God, by Bill Ameiss and Jane Graver (St. Louis: Concordia, 2008)

   Why True Love Waits (the definitive book on how to help your kids resist sexual pressure), by Josh McDowell (Carol Stream, IL: Tyndale, 2002)

   How to Talk Confidently With Your Child About Sex, by Lenore Buth (St. Louis: Concordia, updated and revised, 2008)

   Teaching Your Children Healthy Sexuality, by Jim Burns (Minneapolis: Bethany House, 2008)

   Read and absorb these books, and then talk to your teenager with confidence.

2. Buy one of these books:

   The Purity Code, by Jim Burns (Minneapolis: Bethany House, 2008)

   Love, Sex, and God: Girl's Edition (Learning About Sex series), by Bill Ameiss and Jane Graver (St. Louis: Concordia, 2008)

Love, Sex, and God: For Young Men Ages Fifteen and Up (LEARNING ABOUT SEX series), by Bill Ameiss and Jane Graver (St. Louis: Concordia, 2008)

Read the book first, and then give it to your teenager with love. Pay your teen to read it if you must. Chances are they will be curious, just because the title includes the word *sex*. There are many other good books available as well.

3. Once you are equipped with the information you need, make time to talk to your teenager about what you believe about sexuality and sexual behavior. Don't expect it to be comfortable for either of you, but face it directly for your child's sake.

God, I feel so inadequate to address this subject with my teenager. There is so much I want for this child. Help me to be wise and calm and to accept my child wherever they may be in their knowledge and experience. Prepare my child's heart to hear what I have to say. Amen.

Rebellion and Runaways 10

What is rebellious behavior in a teenager? How does a parent decide if *this* confrontation is an important one? Is it necessary to win every argument with your child? Is it *advisable* to win every argument? If a parent gives in, is he undermining his own authority in the home?

Tough questions. But that doesn't mean they shouldn't be asked. This is a difficult time for moms and dads—transferring authority and responsibility from parents who "always know best" to that "scatterbrained, self-centered, pleasure-bent" kid who seems intent on destroying his life.

To some extent these adult worries may be true. But the fact remains that unless parents want to retain responsibility for their children for the rest of their lives, at some point they will have to relinquish authority.

Handing Over Authority

What does handing over authority have to do with rebellion? Several things. First, one way parents contribute to rebellious behavior in teenagers is to refuse to let them begin to make some decisions for themselves. Some parents think that if they manage their teens' lives and make decisions for them, they will be assuring their adherence to parental values and their teens will be well-behaved. Many of these parents are bewildered to discover that their teens have a powerful will of their own and will not hesitate to use it to get what they want. They may have to bide their time a little before they have the right opportunity. Their determination to do things their own way may be passive or aggressive, but either way it could be labeled rebellious.

Other parents may have been more low-key in their expectations for their children's behavior throughout the childhood years, allowing them to be and do pretty much as they pleased—because it was not disruptive. But suddenly their imaginative teenagers are making behavior choices that are beginning to concern Mom and Dad. Then when parents start to express opinions and override teen decisions, there is war.

Still other parents decide that once their children are teenagers, they should have more freedom—which is the right idea. But they may have failed to give adequate opportunity for their children to grow gradually into responsible decision-making for themselves. In turning over the reins, they find themselves grabbing them back time and again, creating frustration and anger in their fledgling adults.

Charlie Shedd, speaker and writer on parenting, once wrote, "Blessed is the family where children are allowed to become what they can as fast as they can. Blessed also are the parents, who, as fast as they can, will get out of the way!"

It goes without saying that inherent within those words are many years of careful planning and wise management to bring the child to a place of responsible self-government.

Rebellion—A Normal Part of Adolescence?

According to Freudian theory, rebellion against parents is a necessary and inevitable part of normal adolescence. Whether or not one accepts Freud as any kind of reliable authority on normalcy, his view is upheld by many social and psychological scientists.

Other behavioral scientists believe that rebellion occurs only when the adolescent's normal drive for self-determination is frustrated. Children whose parents have consistently facilitated the gradual process toward self-government have little to rebel against.

The adolescent shifts his life more and more into a society of his own. As he starts to feel comfortable in his peer groupings, the family is less satisfying psychologically and has less and less ability to mold him into the desired parental image.

The factors of budding sexuality, growing peer identification, differences in generational thinking and emphasis, and competing authorities certainly pave the way for disagreement between parent and child. But the real question is, "What is the difference between *normal* teenage rebellion and rebellion that is indicative of something more serious—something a parent should be concerned about rather than simply irritated with?"

This is not an easy question to answer because some parents would argue that anything contrary to parental opinion and will is rebellious behavior. These parents would not tolerate even the slightest deviation. Other parents, blissfully ignorant of their child's operations outside of the home, would vehemently defend their child. This child may have learned that the best way to get what he wants is to be sweet and cooperative at home while doing exactly what he wants when free from parental supervision.

Rebellion is defined as resistance against any power or restriction, which means a *rebel* is a person who resists or fights authority instead of obeying it. A further definition describes the rebel as one who *feels* or *exhibits* anger in the face of authority.

Problems for the Rebel

There are several factors motivating the adolescent "rebel." First, he feels the need to find an identity for himself that is separate from his parents. Second, it must be an identity that is acceptable to his peer group. This child wants to establish his independence and his right to make decisions for himself. He attacks anything that smacks of authority in his life with an attitude of criticism, resistance, and belligerence.

When adults take on a firm authoritarian response to his behavior, he vehemently resists. He thus widens the gap between his real need—adult help in getting a good perspective on his life—and his perceived need: total autonomy.

Another definition of teenage rebellion suggests that it is a conscious or unconscious rejection of the values, lifestyle, and/or theology of one's parents. This brings a much narrower approach to the subject of rebellion. While a child may outwardly conform with everything the parent wishes, and all seems smooth and happily under control, there is growing potential for much dissension and conflict. When defiance is blatantly out in the open, the parent at least knows what he is dealing with and can perhaps take steps to bring about understanding.

Too often it is the "ideal" child who suddenly turns the family home into a nightmare as his hostility finally breaks through the quiet exterior and shocks his unsuspecting parents into panicky reactions.

What's a Parent to Do?

It cannot be overemphasized how important parental responses are to the rebellious attitudes and behaviors of their teenagers. When it seems like everything a parent believes in is being attacked by this pre-adult, the natural reaction is to set stronger limits, preach harder "sermons," and more firmly emphasize parental authority. While the rebelling teenager needs limits, he also needs a great deal of positive encouragement to talk out his feelings. Any adult aggression will be met in kind. Parents need to know they cannot talk their child into submissive behavior, nor can they whip him into it. The goal is not broken submission to the will of someone who is stronger. The goal must be to foster a heart change that will allow the teenager to be his own growing-up person, while at the same time maintaining a relationship with the authorities in his life that will contribute in positive ways to his growing independence.

Guidelines for Dealing With Rebellious Behavior

Consider these ten guidelines for dealing with rebellious behavior in your teenager[1]:

1. Do not meet aggressive behavior with aggressive behavior. Although it might create a submissive moment, it also might stimulate more aggression on the part of the teenager that can only lead to trouble.
2. The assertive teenager needs firm controls and definite limits. Think through what is realistic and enforceable. Give him room to maneuver, but be careful not to give in to demands that you disagree with when it comes to moral and safety issues. Encourage him to talk.
3. Don't confront your adolescent in front of his friends or in a group. He will almost certainly be forced to resist in order to save face. And he may receive enough support from his group to make your position impossible.
4. Parental confrontation *must* be characterized by patience and coolness. Take your time. Move slowly. Refuse to be drawn into an argument. Give your teen time to respond. Let periods of silence accentuate the gravity of the situation and your thoughtfulness.
5. Do not touch or make a physically aggressive move toward your adolescent during a confrontation except in self-defense or to prevent injury to your child or someone else.
6. Give your teen time to cool down and think about his behavior. If you are uncertain as to what to do, say so. Let him

1. Adapted from Jack L. Fadely and Virginia N. Hosler, *Confrontation in Adolescence* (St. Louis: The C. V. Mosby Co., 1979).

know you will discuss it as soon as you both have a little time to calm down.

7. Try to give some display of kindness during the "cool down" period. Offer some food, or a soda—any thoughtful gesture that will say you are not happy with this gulf between you. Do not take this moment of angry confrontation as an opportunity to heap discomfort and indignation upon the teenager. Stick to the issue at hand. Be courteous. Don't moralize or preach.
8. Attempt to get a clearly understood verbal commitment about a course of action from the teen, one that is agreed upon and acceptable to both of you.
9. Assure your teen that you have a strong belief in his ability to make the right choices when he has the right kind of information.
10. Recognize that your teenager needs to be becoming more free and able to make his own choices. Try to give him the feeling that he is not being forced into things that are outside of his control, but that he has a voice in what is happening to him.

Your Child's Relationship With God

Parents must recognize that each person's relationship with God is totally personal. We cannot force our Christian convictions and standards upon our children, and we cannot force them into a personal experience with God. We *can* emphasize our desire for conformity in our home, without condemning or chastising our children for their differences with us. We *can* express our concern for their spiritual welfare while at the same time expressing that it is their choice, not ours. And we *can* expect reasonable behavior in accordance with our expressed desires, as long as they choose to live within the protection and financial security of our home. Our children must know that they *will* have total freedom as soon as they are ready to make a go of it themselves. We can let them know that when that time comes, while we may not agree with some of their choices, we will accept them as *their* choices and still love them as our children.

Troublesome Choices

What are some of those choices that give parents trouble? It depends on the personal standards of the parents. They can be anything from abstaining from attending certain movies and listening to secular music to promiscuous sexual conduct. Parents have a responsibility to set the moral code they believe is important for their own home and family. But it is also important to be able to scripturally defend their position to their children and give reasonable reasons for the standards they set.

"Normal" Rebellion vs. Deviant Behavior

When does rebellious behavior become deviant? If we accept that a certain amount of rebellion is normal for teenagers—and we can find ways to live with it even if we don't like it—how do we recognize the danger signals of rebellious behavior that is getting out of control?

Here are some helpful questions proposed by experts in adolescent behavior:

1. Has there been a prolonged period of change in usual eating or sleeping habits (more than a week or two)?
2. Is there a clear change in personality traits? Perhaps your teen is suddenly talkative or withdrawn, morose or excessively cooperative (over a period of one or two weeks or more).
3. Is there a notable change in school performance either socially or academically?
4. Is there a noticeable change in appearance—neat to sloppy or vice versa?

5. Is there an intuitive awareness that something is not right? Some things are not easily definable, but strongly felt by one or the other parent. Pay attention.
6. Are there observable evidences of antisocial behavior—lying, stealing, fighting, or cheating?

If the answer to two or more of these questions is YES, parents ought to seriously confer with each other about the child. It would be helpful to talk with another trusted adult who is knowledgeable about adolescent problems. If all agree that there might be a problem, talk with the child, expressing concern and care for whatever might be troubling him. Let him talk. Do not squelch anything he has to say if he is willing to talk at all. Try to discern the extent of his need, and if you are still worried about his attitude and behavior, consult a professional and get help while the problem is still relatively minor.

Few kids are rebellious without what they consider to be good reasons. Those reasons might not be adequate or objectively valid, but they are their reasons. They will hang on to them in the face of logic or rationality. The best a parent can do is to avoid offering responses that escalate the conflict into an all-out war. However, sometimes war cannot be avoided. The child has firmly and stubbornly set his mind to go his own way without regard to his parents' wishes. His course is set.

Scriptural Warnings

The Bible has many words of warning for children who determine to set themselves against their parents. God does not look lightly upon their behavior. Our children need to know that when they have chosen rebellion, it is no longer just Mom and Dad they are disobeying, but God himself. The teenager may not agree with his parents' standards for him, and he may feel that their expectations are unreasonable. Nevertheless, God has given a commandment specifically to children, apparently for as long as they live under their parents' authority: "Children, obey your parents in the

Lord, for this is right" (Ephesians 6:1 NIV). If they choose disobedience, they are choosing rebellion against God as well.

The Old Testament Jews had a rather drastic solution to the problem of rebellious children. "If someone has a stubborn and rebellious son [*or daughter*] who does not obey his father and mother, and will not listen to them when they discipline him, his father and mother shall take hold of him and bring him to the elders at the gate of his town. They shall say to the elders, 'This son of ours is stubborn and rebellious. He will not obey us. He is a glutton and a drunkard'" (Deuteronomy 21:18–20 NIV, words in italics added). This might be similar to declaring a child "incorrigible," which is allowed in some states. The child is then placed as a ward of the state in an institution or in a group or foster home.

However, the course of action taken in Deuteronomy 21:21 (NIV) was quite certain of bringing the trouble to an end. "Then all the men of his town are to stone him to death." There is no record of this ever occurring in the Scriptures, but the threat was certainly there and evidently kept rebellious children somewhat in line. Perhaps, though, the weak link in carrying out this capital punishment was the parent. For the love of the child, we always bear hope that our child will grow up and change. It happens.

Parents who are experiencing the pain of dealing with wayward children can find much expression of their misery in the book of Proverbs. This indicates that parents throughout history have been forced to live with hurt and agony of soul as it relates to their offspring. "A foolish son brings grief to his father and bitterness to the mother who bore him" (Proverbs 17:25 NIV). Similar sad statements are repeated over and over throughout the book.

The Runaway

Sometimes the rebellious child decides on his own to leave the home without telling his parents. This only escalates the parents' agony. It is reported that between 1.6 and 2.8 million youth between the ages of thirteen and seventeen run away in a given year. Most return home within forty-eight hours to two weeks. Some are found and forcibly returned to their parents' home the same day they leave. Most generally move from one friend's home to another and travel less than ten miles from home. Some are gone longer and travel farther. Some are never seen or heard from again.

There are many reasons kids run away. Typically, running away is an impulsive reaction to a conflict at home. Some of the reasons teens give include feelings of not belonging, not feeling good enough for their mom and dad, parents fighting or getting a divorce, problems with stepparents or step-siblings, a parent's alcohol or drug abuse, physical or sexual abuse, peer influence, being bullied at school, fear of gangs, and moving to a new area and/or school. There are undoubtedly as many reasons as there are kids. But at the bottom of all the reasons is usually a significant lack of family communication.

Running away may be seen by the teenager as a way to achieve independence or at least make a strong, angry statement against his parents' rules and unwillingness to relax restrictions. Most runaways want to return home and expect their parents to look for them. They are saying, "Listen to me! Give me what I want! Or at least hear me out."

Most runaways are fifteen- to seventeen-year-olds. For those who do not return home within the first few days, life can get very hard. The sixteen-year-old who leaves home with $100 in his pocket may think he has all he needs to take care of himself indefinitely. He soon finds out his estimation of his own needs was way too low. When the money is gone, the choices become narrow. He can return home, find friends who will help him, or find a way to make some quick money.

For the young person who is determined not to go home, or fears going home, the alternatives may become theft, prostitution, or peddling drugs. Most runaways who are serious head for the "big city" with every intention of making it just fine. But reality sets in all too soon.

Our own rebellious runaway left four times for extended "adventures." Twice he came home of his own accord after he was convinced he *could* come home. Twice he ended up in jail. There were many other times he left home without permission. He was lucky. Some of the stories he has related to us about his runaway and rebellious episodes give me panicked feelings even now. They are clear evidence of God's protective hand on his life.

It becomes immediately obvious to the mom and dad of a runaway that no matter how difficult the situation was at home, it was preferable to the pounding feelings of terror that threaten to crush the heart as we imagine all manner of evil enveloping our child.

The first time our son left home he took our second car, which was being used by him and his brother. He also took his father's rifle and, as far as we knew, very little money. It is impossible to describe the physical pain that courses through your body as your mind runs wild and imagines every possible terrible thing that could happen.

My concern was for his emotional stability. The event that led him to leave seemed to have made him emotionally distraught. My husband's fear was that in order to meet his needs, he might be driven to do something foolish like robbery. I feared he might take his life. As we cried together in prayer for this child, we opened the Bible and begged God for some word of comfort or help.

My Bible fell open to Isaiah 51, and my eyes fell immediately to verse 14: "The captive exile and he who is bent down by chains shall speedily be released; and he shall not die and go down to the pit of destruction, nor shall his food fail."

With one verse of Scripture, God had answered both our fears. We relaxed a little. But God's "speedy release" didn't come for four days. By the second day we knew where he was. A couple from our church ran into him in Seattle. They didn't know he had run away from home. In the course of a long-distance phone conversation with a mutual friend, they casually mentioned seeing him. This friend relayed the message to us. They didn't know he had left home either. It was just a chance comment during our conversation, and another way God had provided.

The Parents' Reaction

When parents live through a runaway episode they immediately lose the illusion that they can control their child. Until that moment, they may cling to the tiniest belief that they really can make this child "knuckle under" if they take the time, say the right words, and act firmly. Not so. All attempts have only worsened the situation. They are at the bottom of the barrel.

At this point, parents suffer much self-blame, guilt, and remorse. There may be a tendency to think all their standards and restrictions were unreasonable. Or they may have the opposite reaction, throwing all the blame on the child and his rebellious, stubborn behavior. Some parents try to assuage their own guilty feelings with fixing blame elsewhere. Maybe the pastor or the youth leaders will receive their share of blame as the mom and dad desperately try to handle their own emotional ravages by hurling their self-anger at someone else.

What to Do When Your Teenager Runs Away

What should a parent do if he suspects, or knows, his child has run away? If it appears obvious that clothing has been taken or items are missing that indicate your teen plans to go somewhere and stay awhile, immediately call around to relatives or friends to see if they might have seen the teen or have any information since the suspected time of leaving.

If that fails to turn up anything, a few phone calls to your teenager's friends or their parents might provide some clues. Many runaways leave with a companion. You may find someone else who is missing from their home.

If school is in session, call to see if he showed up for school, which will help narrow down what time of day he may have started his escapade. Check at the local bus or train station. Take along a picture of your child.

Check with your local police department. They may not take any action—they receive many reports of runaways or missing teenagers. They know that most return home in a day or two, so they are not likely to take any action until they are fairly certain this is a true runaway. But you *should* go to the police and make whatever report you are allowed to make at that time. There is also the possibility an abduction has taken place. They will know what to do.

If the child has taken some family belongings of value, or a vehicle, a warrant for the child's arrest could be filed. This might speed police action *if* this is what parents feel they must do. The danger of this action is that the child, already feeling rejected and unloved, might decide that the only reason his parents went looking for him was to "get the car back."

It is also frightening to think of what a confrontation with police might be like for an angry, scared teenager.

When Your Teenager Is Found

What happens when the runaway is located but refuses to come home? If parents can communicate their desire to have him come home and work things out without preaching, punishment, and condemnation, he may change his mind and make the voluntary decision to return.

One parent received a phone call from another parent in a distant town. The runaway had shown up at their home to "visit" his old friend from summer camp days. The friend's parents were suspicious because it was during a school day, and the runaway had traveled 400 miles to "visit." So she made the young man comfortable, fed him some lunch, and without his knowledge called his parents to make sure everything was OK. She discovered she was harboring a runaway.

The wise mother confronted the runaway gently and gave him the message that his parents were worried sick about him. They cared for him. They wanted him to come home. She also made it clear that if he chose not to go home, he couldn't stay in her home. He agreed to let his parents come pick him up.

When the Runaway Comes Home

When parents and teen come together again, it is not the time to review bad behavior and how much it cost to get him home. It is a time to be sure this child knows how much he is loved and wanted. It is time to review the reasons he felt he had to run away.

It is time for the parents to decide if they can live with this teenager, even temporarily, if he is still hostile and unwilling to accept the family rules. Was this a manipulative gesture to get his way?

On the other hand, it is not weakness for the parent to admit they may have been too harsh or demanding. It is not weakness to apologize and say you're sorry for the distress. But it *is* weakness to acquiesce to the teenager's demands or tears, and let go of your values and standards. One of the comments made by our wayward son after he had his life together was, "You and Dad made me so mad all the time. You wouldn't budge on what you thought was important. Thank you."

Be Careful of the "Lessons You Teach"

Your teenager needs to know that you love him too much to let him get away with truly rebellious behavior. But don't make the mistake of "teaching him a lesson." Friends in our church family, believing they were doing the right thing, turned their fifteen-year-old daughter's bedroom into a sewing room when she ran away for a week to a relative's home. They packed her things in boxes and put them in the garage. Their intention was to show her that if she could reject them, they could reject her. They wanted her to feel bad and come home. They wanted her to experience the same kind of hurt they were experiencing. When her parents didn't call to beg her to come home, and her older brother told her what had become of her room and her things, she was angry and hurt. She called their bluff and never returned home. She moved in with several older girls also searching for independence from parental rules. She dropped out of school. She didn't get heavily involved in the drug and alcohol scene, but she did become sexually promiscuous. She found guys would pay her to have sex, and since she was only fifteen, it was the only "job" she could find. At nineteen, she had had two abortions, had a minimum-wage job, and a distant relationship with her parents. Her mother wondered often, with tears, about what might have been.

Another family we know had trouble with their fourteen-year-old son. His rebellion consisted of being too lazy to follow through with chores and keep up his part in helping with family responsibilities. After several loud and long confrontations, he left home for several days. When his parents discovered where he was, they forcibly brought him home to talk things over. They decided to use the tactic that if he would not accept responsibility for family chores and help when asked, he could not participate in family activities. When he would come to join the family for table games or TV watching, they would exclude him with the remark that if he didn't want to be part of the family, it was his choice; please leave. His mother would not set a place for him at the table if he failed to complete his chores. They planned a family weekend vacation, purposely excluding him because he hadn't completed appointed tasks.

He ran away again. After several days they found him, but this time, after considering my counsel and the counsel of their pastor, they decided to work at making this child feel loved and accepted rather than giving him the impression that only by acceptable behavior could he have any worth in the family. They were also counseled to make sure he performed his chores, even if Mom or Dad had to physically walk him through them. The family worked hard at giving their child acceptance and love—and boundaries. He didn't run away again. Today, he is a responsible husband and father.

It is never too late to let your child know you love him. A youth leader we heard speaking at a family camp said there are only two really important things when it comes to parent-child relationships: (1) Your child loves you; and (2) he is alive! With those two realities, parents and children have the potential to work through any problems they might have.

The Parents' Self-Awareness

Living with rebellion in the home is heart-wrenching. But if it is the reality in your home, you must learn to deal with it in a way that will eventually win your child back. This means that parents sometimes have to grow up a little, too. We may have to set aside some of our attitudes of "parental rights" and "total power and authority." We may even have to set aside our own reasonable desires for our children's future and acknowledge *their* right to plan their own lives.

Parents need to understand that their children need freedom to explore the new areas of life that are opening up to them. Freedom does need boundaries, but those boundaries must be set in love and reason, with the health and growth of the child as the focus.

Listen to the wisdom of the Scriptures: "Do not provoke or irritate or fret your children [do not be hard on them or harass them], lest they become discouraged and sullen and morose and feel inferior and frustrated. [Do not break their spirit]" (Colossians 3:21).

Something to Do

1. Mom, Dad, sit down together and discuss what behaviors are unacceptable to you. This may include underage drinking, experimentation with illegal (or even legal) drugs, or other ways of getting "high." It may also include provocative dress, inappropriate sexual behavior, questionable friends, or exclusive dating relationships. When you agree, and have reasons in place that support your decisions, write these down as a reminder of the things you will stand firm on.

2. On a separate piece of paper, make a list of things you want for this child, remembering that some things you want may not be on the child's list of things he wants for himself. This list might include some of the tasks teenagers need to address before leaving the comfort and safety of their family's home. It might also include positive statements about what the child *is* achieving (without the "but . . .").

3. Invite your teen out for pizza or another meal at a favorite restaurant, telling him that you want to talk about some important things that will help make living in your home together a good experience for the remainder of his high

school years. Tell him you want to hear what he has to say, and yes, you will listen. Remind him it doesn't mean you will agree, but you do want to hear what he is thinking.

4. Remind your child that you love him. Remind him that you know the teen years can be a struggle. You know that parents seem to be the enemy sometimes. Ask the child to trust you to want the best for him. Let him know you may make mistakes, and ask him to forgive you in advance. Let him know he can say what he needs to say and be safe. Invite him to write you notes if it is too difficult to speak face-to-face. Promise you will not go ballistic at whatever he writes or says. Keep that promise.

5. Suggest other adults he may talk to if he feels you are not hearing him. Suggest that maybe a counselor who works with and understands teenagers might be helpful—maybe there are some things he cannot comfortably share with his parents, but it would be worth talking with someone who will honor his confidentiality and give him some helpful feedback or suggestions. Offer to set up an appointment anytime he might choose, with no questions asked.

6. Gently insist that this child be a part of the family commitment to go to church together. He doesn't have to like it. He doesn't have to participate in activities he doesn't care for, but he will go to church with the family as long as he is in the home. You may or may not say this, but it is important that there is a voice of reason counterbalancing the other voices this child is hearing. If there is no voice of reason in your church, perhaps it is time to find another church.

7. If nothing seems to be working, or even if things seem to be better, it still might be wise to make an appointment with a family therapist and talk out your concerns. Ask around. Hopefully there is someone in your community you will be able to trust to help you get through the teenage years without having the heartache of a teenage runaway.

8. If your child runs away, follow through with all the steps mentioned within this chapter to get him home.

Dear God of the sons and daughters of our hearts, please protect them from themselves during this transitioning time of their lives. Thank you for trusting us with this child. Help us to show him love and acceptance. Help us to be strong in our commitment to what we believe is right. Help us sort out what is reasonable from the unreasonable. Amen.

Have We Done Anything Right? 11

The following paragraphs are in our son Steve's own words:

I remember that night clearly. I was racing another kid down a city street at 63 mph right past a cop. My first thought was: *What a stupid way to end up in jail.* I had a small baggie of pot on me, and a pipe under my car seat. I was delivering a "substance" to another guy. Fortunately for me, the substance turned out to be a fake so they couldn't charge me with that. But what I had done was enough to write my ticket to prison. I had been warned by the judge, by my probation officer, by my parents, and even by a few friends. I didn't hear them.

I was mad at everybody who wouldn't let me just do what I wanted to do when I wanted to do it. Just leave me alone. If I couldn't finance what I wanted to do, I could write a check or pawn something or steal something. All at someone else's expense, but that didn't seem to register with me. I had been through some pretty rough stuff, but it didn't deter me.

The weird thing was I felt a strange sense of relief at being caught again. For a while I had been wondering when I was going to have to "pay." It looked like *now* was the time. Deep inside, I knew, *Now I can't hurt anybody anymore, can't hurt myself—for a long time.* I *was* remorseful, but I was always looking for a quick fix. I was looking for a place to *belong,* like I was. I found places, but they were never satisfying.

My urging to parents is, *never* stop doing the right thing. You have nothing to feel guilty about. Your kid is the one making all of the wrong choices. If you keep patching up his consequences, it will just take longer for him, or her, to get it together, or they may never get it together. They need to feel the sting of the consequences for their choices. Remind yourselves, if you have instilled good things—*any* good things—they *will* make a difference. Do examine yourselves. If you have been wrong in some ways, admit it. Confess it to your teenager. But, never give up. Never stop praying. Believe that God will do His thing, and your child *will* change, eventually.

Remember, there was nothing anybody could have said to me at that time that would have made a difference. I was determined. My advice to your teenager is, Man up. Grow up. Realize there are people who love you and will do anything to get you on the right track. Parents, be hard. Stand strong for what you know is right.

Standing Strong

Parents, stand up for your beliefs. Hold on to your convictions. Do not let the enemy steal your child—or your own peace of mind and sanity. Remember the things you have done right. And remember God's command given directly to children: "Honor your father and mother" (Exodus 20:12). That is their responsibility. Ours is to teach them how to do it.

Maybe you messed up. Maybe you were too strict or unreasonable. Maybe you were too lenient, too accommodating, or too fearful of your child not liking you. Maybe you did everything as right as you knew how, given your own upbringing and understanding. We don't know it all when we begin the journey with our children. Both they and we suffer for it. But we learn as we grow older, and if you haven't learned yet, know that *it's never too late* to acknowledge your failure *to* your child and say, "I'm sorry, please forgive me. Let's get it right from here on."

Humbleness, not humiliation, is the way to restore relationships. It's about recognizing and acknowledging mistakes, choices you wish you could take back, dreams that didn't turn out as you hoped. Bring these first to the Savior, and let Him rebuild the broken places.

Isaiah 61:1–3 gives us hope and a promise. "The Spirit of the Lord God is upon me . . . to bind up and heal the brokenhearted . . . to comfort all who mourn . . . to grant [consolation and joy] . . . to give them an ornament (a garland or diadem) of beauty instead of ashes, the oil of joy instead of mourning, the garment [expressive] of praise instead of a heavy, burdened, and failing spirit—that they may be called oaks of righteousness [lofty, strong, and magnificent, distinguished for uprightness, justice, and right standing with God], the planting of the Lord, that *He* might be glorified" (emphasis added).

None of us has done it *all* right. But remember the things you know you did in order to help this child grow up and have some sense of right and wrong. Don't apologize for being "old-fashioned." Do apologize for getting caught up in this world's version of what's right and letting your standards slide.

Step back a little. Decide how you are going to address some of your child's intolerable behaviors. If you haven't done things right before, start doing them that way now.

It's Never Too Late

You may be thinking it's too late. That you've already messed up more than you can fix. Maybe you're not living with your teenager's biological dad. Maybe it's the third man in the house, or more. Maybe you're feeling hopeless. You think your kid is messed up because of the choices *you* made. Be encouraged. *It's never too late*. Find a tender moment. Tell your teenager you love him. Tell him you are sorry he has been hurt by choices you have made. You can't change the choices, but you want him to know that you are going to do things differently from now on.

Give your child the message that she must show respectful behavior to her stepparent. She cannot talk to him or her the way she has any longer. As the biological parent you may not have allowed the stepparent to interfere, to punish or correct bad behavior, or to help with teaching and disciplining this child. You can't undo that. You can't put the stepparent in a place of authority now and expect your teenager to accept it. But you can expect and require decent, respectful behavior in response to adult authority.

Our children must learn to respect and obey authority. All their lives they will have authority figures—teachers, supervisors, bosses, committee chairmen, and the law—they will need to obey. If they don't learn this at the parental level, they *will* learn it at another level. They may lose promotions or jobs. They may get C's instead of A's. They may not be able to go out with friends on a weekend. They may lose their cell phone for a week. They may go to jail. It doesn't matter if they like the rules. They will pay a price for ignoring or flagrantly breaking them.

Of course we also need to train our children to recognize when an authority is asking or telling them to do something morally wrong or damaging. Sometimes they will have to make choices to uphold their own moral code. They may choose to take a D rather than violate their own sense of truth. They may quit a job because of what they cannot do in good conscience.

Three Life Rules—Only Three

No matter what we have done right or wrong, we can start fresh. As a parent-education instructor for several years with a community college, I worked with teachers and parents in cooperative preschools. These preschools had three rules. Only three. They were explained to the two- through five-year-olds at the beginning of each preschool year, and referred to often as the year progressed:

1. I won't do anything that would hurt me.
2. I won't do anything that would hurt someone else.

3. I won't do anything to hurt (damage or destroy) the things I play with that give me fun and make me happy.

These are, in essence, the basic rules of life. They are the basic tenets of the Scriptures. Consciously, or unconsciously, we parents are teaching our children these things from their infancy. Do we do it perfectly? No. Could we do it better? Undoubtedly. But most of us do the best we can with the level of awareness and knowledge we have.

We ask, wouldn't it have been better for us and for our children if God had let us grow up a bit before He put that helpless, dependent little baby in our laps? But that question misses something important. The truth is we are motivated to grow up *because* we have that tiny, helpless child. Sometimes we resist. We bring too many of our own childhood or adult hurts to the responsibility. We don't follow the basic rules of life. And we learn. In many ways, parents and children grow each other up. That's a good thing.

When to Seek Professional Help

When our children are physically ill, we are nearly frightened out of our minds, but at least we can do something. We can seek medical help. We can find a course of treatment, and hopefully our child will get well. Or if it's a chronic illness, we learn to manage.

But what if your child's brain and emotional world is out of sorts? How do you know? Who will help? The world of mental health has made great strides in the last few decades. Many children are being diagnosed with disorders that can be treated, and their lives are changed for the better. But how do you *know* this is what needs to be done? I wish there were an easy answer, but the truth is there are no laboratory tests, no definitive physiological evaluations that can give us all the answers we seek.

The best place to begin is to know and understand normal child development patterns and the best parental response to the developing person at various stages of growth. If your child is or has been far enough outside of the norm to cause concern or conflict, or if there has been poor peer interaction at any age, don't ignore it or look the other way. Don't accuse the teacher if your child is failing in school. Don't accept as normal uncontrollable temper tantrums, whether at home or in public. Don't just assume all kids his age act like that, or do that or think like that. It may or may not be true, but if it's unhealthy, immoral, disrespectful, or destructive, it's a problem and needs to be addressed.

If these behaviors have been a fairly consistent part of life with this child, seek help. Teachers are not supposed to be mental health experts, but it's a place to start. Talk to your school counselor. They should have advice, or a resource they can refer you to. Also, find out what your school district offers in the way of testing and/or services your child might qualify for.

If you feel brushed aside or think you are not being taken seriously, seek and find a child/adolescent psychologist or a licensed child specialist in private practice. Take your concerns there. Ask for testing. Be prepared to pay—a lot. You may have insurance that will pay part of the costs, but even if you don't, consider the relatively small cost of psychological testing compared to having your child drop out of school or become an alcoholic, or of having a child with learning difficulties that were never diagnosed. Maybe a child psychiatrist, as a last resort, can help discover psychological issues that prevent this child from succeeding.

However, given the bent of our society, many children are just confused. Their homes may be in disarray, and so are they. They may be depressed, anxious, fearful—and as a result they act out.

Words of Respect

One obvious sign of the growing gulf between parent and child is shown in the way they talk to one another. Rarely does disrespectful language appear out of nowhere with a rebellious teenager. More often, parents have allowed their child to use inappropriate language for some time when conversing or arguing with them.

And sometimes parents use inappropriate language in dealing with their child!

A parent came to talk with me about her fifteen-year-old daughter. She was "sick to death" of her daughter's foul mouth and disrespectful behavior. They went to church as a family, and the daughter was active in the church youth group. Everyone seemed to like her there, but at home she was obnoxious. I asked, "How long has this been going on?" "For years!" the mother replied. "I just can't take it anymore." I asked why she had allowed it up until now. She looked puzzled, and then said, "Well, it didn't seem so bad at first, but she's getting worse, and using really bad language. I don't know if she does it away from home. I can't imagine she would, but she sure lets it go on us."

As we discussed it further, she acknowledged that she and her husband occasionally used some pretty explicit words themselves when pushed to their limits. In essence, they had been telling her it's OK to use bad language when you're upset or angry about something, and they had reinforced it by allowing her to use those words to express her unhappiness. Now, at fifteen, she was turning these words on her parents—the people she perceived as the source of her frustration and anger. And she had picked up a few more choice words from her peer group, movies, and TV.

Parents, it's time to own up. The next time your teenager mouths off at you, don't say anything at all for a moment. Then say, "You know, we all use too many words like that. I'm tired of hearing them from you, and I know you're tired of hearing them from me. Let's change it. What do you suggest?"

There's a good chance you won't get a decent response. But you might be surprised. Either way, in a quiet, in-control manner, say, "Well, here's what I'm going to do about it. I'll talk to you when each of us is in a better mood." Then leave. You may be followed. The anger and disrespect may still be at the top of your teen's mind. Then you can tell her once again, "Come to me when you're done being angry and disrespectful, and we'll talk about it then." There may be more conversation about the matter. Keep your cool, and refuse to get engaged in an angry confrontation. If it is dropped, wait a day or two (or an hour or two, depending on how often your teen "goes off"), and approach the subject again.

In a relatively serene moment, approach your teen. "I'd like for us to talk." Even if there isn't a response, talk anyway. "Please hear what I have to say. The bad language and disrespectful behaviors have to stop. I'm guilty, too. I know it. I will make a determined effort to stop using disrespectful words, and I expect you to do so as well. This is what we will do."

One idea is to have a jar in which you place some money. Tell your teenager they may spend any money that is left in the jar on Friday night after dinner (or any time you choose). Start the jar with $5 (or $10, or $20—you know your teen's mouth). The plan is that every time Mom or Dad uses bad language, they put $1 in the jar. Every time the teen uses foul language or shows disrespectful behavior, $1 comes out of the jar and back to the parent. Make a list of the words that will not be acceptable. Put the list inside the jar. You may need to add words to the list as they come up.

You can mention to your teen that if this doesn't work, you have other ideas. But put forward just one idea at a time. Remind your teen you have more stringent rules in mind, but you don't want to go there yet. That's all they need to know.

It's important that Mom and Dad do this *together,* for everyone's benefit.

Taking Personal Responsibility

Dr. Phil McGraw, in his book *Relationship Rescue*, states that we have the ability to change the relationships in our lives by acknowledging *our* part in bringing about negative behavior in others. Change can happen when we ask ourselves the following questions:[2]

1. Am *I* doing something that is bringing about this action/reaction? I need to examine my own words, actions, and motives.

2. Adapted from Dr. Phil McGraw, *Relationship Rescue: A Seven-Step Strategy for Reconnecting With Your Partner* (New York: Hyperion, 2000).

Have I consciously or unconsciously set a fire, making my teen feel accused, threatened, or thwarted in some way?

2. Am *I* "keeping it going?" My teenager may have started a conflict with his disrespectful behavior, but I need to let it go. I am angry. I am threatened. I am accused. But I don't need to have the last word.

3. Have I given up? Am I allowing my teen's behavior to go on and on? If I am powerless, everyone *loses*. Especially my teenager.

So have we done *anything* right? Probably. But regardless of what has been done, today is a new day. If you've done a lot of things right, build on those things. If you feel you've done nothing right (for the record, you're probably wrong), start doing right today. Forgive yourself. Do what you can. It's never too late to do the right things, with the right attitude, for the right reasons.

Remember, *you* can't change your teenager. You can try but will likely fail miserably. You *can* change yourself. And when we parents change in the right ways, with the right attitude, for the right reasons, our teenagers will eventually respond differently. They may react and push back, but if you fiercely hold on to what's right, something will change. Be prepared.

Something to Do

1. List five things you know you have done right as parents. Why do you think these things were right?

2. List three things you know you need to apologize for to your teenager. Tell him or her *why* you are apologizing. Ask her to forgive you. Commit to changing your own behavior.

3. Consider making a Job Jar as an incentive for better behavior. Choose fifteen to twenty small jobs or chores, or small increments of bigger jobs (i.e., dust all shelves in the family room, clean the toilets, clean the inside of the car—instructions

included—don't assume your teenager should know how to do the job). Assign a dollar amount to each task. When your teenager chooses to "ignore" a family rule, he must pick a chore from the Job Jar and do it before any social interaction, texting, phone calls, etc., or maybe before bedtime. You know what works for your child. Be consistent. Be fair. Be matter-of-fact. No pay is involved with this consequence. But if your teenager wants money for something, give him the opportunity to earn it by picking a job from the jar. He can choose which job to do. Money has to be earned. It can also be given as a gift, but it's important for our teenager to know the difference. So the Job Jar serves two functions: it is a consequence for unacceptable behavior (no choice, no pay), or an income source. If your child refuses to comply, take away social events. Hold out. Don't argue or threaten or label. If he chooses to rebel in more troublesome ways, quietly remind him he is making the choices. All he has to do is follow through with what you have previously discussed, and all will be well again. It's up to him.

4. When your teen comes home after the agreed-upon time, let him know that next time he is late he has to come in twice that amount of time early the next time out. In other words, if he's half an hour late, he has to come in an hour earlier next time. If he doesn't honor that, he doesn't go out the next time he asks—no matter what it is. You may want to exclude church or sports commitments, reminding him that these commitments involve other people in ways that teach us to be faithful and responsible.

5. Help your teenager to "own his own stuff." Remind him, kindly, to pick up the paper scraps, candy wrappers, and soda cans, and toss them; and then take his dirty dishes to the sink or the dishwasher. If he does these things without grumbling, thank him. If he grumbles, remind him that could be a Job Jar offense—does he want to risk it? Give him a warning or two, then pick from the jar. If he leaves clothes

or personal items lying around, suggest he get in the habit of putting these things in their proper places so they won't get lost, broken, or confiscated (by you). Be consistent. When you confiscate things, don't hide them. Just make it inconvenient to retrieve them. What if they don't care? They will, eventually.

6. Determine today, with your parent partner, to make positive changes to bring more peace and less open conflict into your home. There are no guaranteed ways to reach your teenager. But there are things you can do and say that have the potential to make a difference. Don't just say, "It won't work with my child," until you've tried it. And if nothing works, the last chapter of this book may help you find your personal peace in a trying circumstance.
7. If you suspect there could be a biological reason your teenager is having difficulty, talk to someone soon. Seek the advice of a professional. Don't delay. Don't get your teenager involved until you have good information to work with.

Prayer

Dear God, the author of right, help me do what I must do to give my child what he needs to succeed and find a good place in his life. Teach me how to be humble and quiet inside and to examine myself. I ask you to continue to speak to my child's heart. Teach him what only you can teach. Amen.

Keeping It Together When It Gets Bad 12

The heavy iron door slammed behind me with a thud. I looked down the long dingy hall lined with other iron doors. Iron doors with bars everywhere. This was the county jail. My son was behind one of those doors.

This was the third time he had been jailed. He had already spent ninety days here, and now he faced two years for probation violation and forgery.

For several years we had tried one thing after another. We had sought counsel from the church, from juvenile authorities, from professional counselors, from anyone we thought might be able to give us some answers. There were no answers—or at least none that we could find to help us in our desperation.

Hopelessness vs. Trust

There were moments of feeling totally helpless. There was nothing we could do. This child we loved was bent on his own destruction, and we didn't know how to change his direction.

In my feelings of dreadful aloneness and frustration, I lashed out at God. He was the only hope we had, but where was He? Many times I would open my Bible begging for some help just to make it through one more day. I felt the futility of it all when I read the exchange between Jesus and His disciples when He asked them, "Do you also want to go away?" The men replied, "Lord, to whom shall we go? You have the words of eternal life" (John 6:67–68 NKJV). Instead of being buoyed by the truth that Jesus *was* the reality of life here, and the life to come, I was angry that He didn't seem to care enough to save my son from the awful circumstances he was in.

I believed. Even in my most down moments, I still believed. But wrapped up in the believing was a kind of hopelessness that made me feel I was at God's mercy. Maybe He didn't really care all that much about what I was going through.

Then the light began to dawn. I started to realize that I wasn't thinking so much about my son's predicaments and rebellion as I was about how God could do this to *me*. How could He let me suffer so much after all I'd done for Him?

It was unnerving for me to face the fact that in spite of what I knew from the Bible, in spite of what I preached to others and gently reminded grieving parents about, I still believed that God should keep a neat little hedge of protection around my family. I knew dreadful things happened to other Christians and their families, but I really didn't expect anything bad to happen to me or to mine.

I had to face my own self-righteousness as God reminded me of my quiet, veiled judgments upon other families who had experienced troubles with their teenagers. I realized I knew very little about God's eternal purposes, and my thinking was all tied up with the here and now—the things of this earth. I wanted everything to be nice and happy now. I didn't want to have to deal with uncomfortable things, painful things. I wanted God to give me a rose-garden existence. And, I was angry at Him for the rain and the thorns.

The rebellion began early with our son. When he was almost eight years old, I begged the Lord to give me a Scripture to hang on to. There had been some particularly worrisome events, and

I was upset and concerned that this child might find more and more mischief to entertain himself with. In tears, I opened my King James Bible to read: "My Spirit that is upon thee, and my words which I have put in thy mouth, shall not depart out of thy mouth, nor out of the mouth of thy seed, nor out of the mouth of thy seed's seed, saith the Lord, from henceforth and for ever" (Isaiah 59:21).

I had no idea at that time that many years later I would be clinging desperately to those words, reminding God over and over that He had promised me that my rebellious boy was going to be His child—and not only him, but all my children, and all my grandchildren, and more. I believe God gave me a truth to hold on to; and whether I see it in this life or not, that message sustains me.

The book of Isaiah became a treasure trove of promises and encouragements. The prophet seemed to know my heart. "Who is among you who [reverently] fears the Lord . . . yet who walks in darkness and deep trouble and has no shining splendor [in his heart]? Let him rely on, trust in, and be confident in the name of the Lord, and let him lean upon and be supported by his God" (50:10).

In the New Testament, Peter shared the example of Jesus, who was perfect and sinless yet suffered the agony of unjust treatment that finally took Him to the cross. We are told that He took it all, suffering silently, not offering insults in return, and not making any threats. He trusted His Father to do what was right (1 Peter 2:21–23). This is a reminder that we, being imperfect, and perhaps reaping the outcomes of some of our own choices, should not expect to be treated better in this life than our Savior was, or feel worthy of a "bliss-filled" life.

"Without faith it is impossible to please [God]" (Hebrews 11:6). Without faith, it is barely possible to keep our heads above water during troubled times. The Bible tells us that faith comes by hearing and gaining an understanding of the Word of God (Romans 10:17).

I talked with an upset mother of a rebellious teenager during a time of heavy stress. She looked at me almost accusingly and said, "It's easy for you to trust God to work everything out. You've been a Christian a long time."

Yes, I had been a Christian a long time. And yes, during that time I had seen God do some wonderful things—for others and for my own family. But one important thing I was learning through this experience with our son was that you can never store up enough faith and trust to see you through the hard times. Our faith in God, our trust in His ability to carry us and our loved ones through difficult times, is a daily, moment-by-moment relationship with our heavenly Father.

I shared with this heartsick mother that she had every resource I had. The only strength I found to meet each day was the strength I found in Christ as I met Him daily to receive assurance and love and trust-building encouragement.

I was aware through reading the Bible that if there was any hope for our son, it was only to be found in God. And through reading God's Word I was assured that I could trust Him, in His time, to make all things right.

It was necessary for me to come to the realization that my son had to face his own responsibility directly before God. He was rebelling and caught in the mesh of his choices, and he was going to have to make it right with God—alone. It became a little easier to bear when I finally settled on the fact that our son was choosing to reject God's moral law that he knew and had been taught. It took some of the load off of us, his parents, and made reconciliation God's responsibility.

We had made plenty of mistakes. But in confessing our lack of rightness and asking our son's forgiveness, we had freed ourselves from much of the guilt-ridden responsibility we had felt. The job was now God's and His alone. We knew we were incapable of doing anything more, and God had promised to see us through.

Resignation vs. Acceptance

Job, a saint of God in the Old Testament, was surely a man tried and tested to the very limits of his endurance. He lost his wealth, his possessions, his family, and finally his physical health. He is often spoken of as a man of righteousness, patience, and faithfulness to God in spite of his circumstances.

The things Job said when he was going through his trials really touched my heart as a grieving parent of a rebellious child: "[Why is the light of day given] to a man (*parent*) whose way is hidden, and whom God has hedged in? . . . My sighing comes before my food . . . my groanings are poured out like water. . . . For the thing which I greatly fear comes upon me. . . . I . . . am not at ease, nor . . . have I rest, nor . . . am I quiet. . . . Trouble came and still comes" (Job 3:23–26, word in italics in parentheses added).

I was painfully aware that my commitment to God was tainted with the attitude that He could have everything there was of me; ask all He would; send me anywhere He willed—as long as He didn't touch my children. There was the slightest unspoken "deal" in the depths of my heart. If I was *this* faithful, surely my children would be safe and whole all the days of their lives. Life would move smoothly along, and I would praise God for the beauty of each day.

How deceived we can become! We forget there is a much bigger battle being waged—a spiritual war in which each Christian plays a part. We have an enemy who is out to destroy our peace and undermine our trust in God. When we finally determine that God is in control no matter how bad things get, we very often end up with the same poor attitude Job had: "As God lives, Who has taken away my right and denied me justice, and the Almighty, Who has vexed me and embittered my life" (Job 27:2). "God has cast me into the mire. . . . I cry to You, [Lord], and You do not answer me; I stand up, but You [only] gaze [indifferently] at me. You have become harsh and cruel to me; with the might of Your hand You [keep me alive only to] persecute me" (Job 30:19–21). With Job, we take the attitude that God can and will do anything He pleases, and we must suffer with it—an attitude of *resignation*.

We give up. "I am in God's hands and there is nothing I can do about it." It is a feeling of defeat, perhaps even hopelessness. Things may get better or they may get worse, but there is nothing I can do about it. God is in control.

We need to understand there is nothing noble or good about this kind of resignation. It implies that we have been fighting and now realize we have lost. We surrender in bitterness and weariness. We wait for the enemy to do with us what he will, with God's approval.

God wants something better for us. There is no peace in mere resignation. Peace comes when we begin to understand the master plan of God for His children. Romans 8:28 is well-known: "And we know that all things work together for good to them that love God, to them who are the called according to his purpose" (KJV). The trouble is, most of us believe this verse is saying, "Everything is going to turn out OK; every cloud has a silver lining"!

Romans 8:29 brings light and context by telling us God has a master purpose for each of His children—to mold us into the image of His Son, that inwardly we may be like Him. These verses are not saying that if we behave, He will see to it that every story has a happy ending. He *is* assuring us that in spite of the painful, traumatic, even calamitous things that may come into our lives, we can find peace and a joy that is beyond explanation. These experiences will help deepen our sense of identification with Christ and change us into better persons if we accept them for that purpose.

I've heard it said that every problem we encounter in life will make us either bitter or better. God wants us to be better.

Whenever we are faced with a situation that hits us directly in the pit of the stomach and threatens to squeeze the life out of us, we have essentially three choices: (1) We can get uptight, angry, and distraught, and lash out at everything around us, including God. (2) We can give up in resignation to the God who will do what He wills regardless of our needs or desires. (3) We can believe that God loves us dearly and has good reasons for allowing our difficult circumstances. My child needs to learn some things. I have to learn some things. Others may be affected, but the ultimate reason for our circumstances is to give us a place to grow. This is *acceptance*. It is alive, active, and assertive.

The Bible tells us the rain falls on the just and the unjust alike. We are subject to anything and everything that can happen in this world, and our children are not hedged about with an automatic wall of protection. We can love them, train them in right ways, and teach them about God, but they will make their own choices. If we have laid good foundations they will most likely come back to us stronger persons. But even if the foundations we have built under our children are less than adequate, there is still hope. As Mom and Dad develop a stronger and more secure faith in God, their growing stability will have a drawing power that will reach out to that wayward child and draw him back.

Panic vs. Peace

Acceptance brings peace—an infinitely precious and infinitely valuable gift from God. In the desperate hurt that never seems to go away, we long for peace. But the kind of peace we are looking for is very different from the peace God is offering. We ask for freedom from the battles and the arguments. We beg for quiet and rest from the tension.

But the peace of God isn't only the end of strife. It is a calm assurance, a settled knowledge, even though it might be shaky, that God is in control. It is an awareness that nothing can happen to me or mine that He does not allow. And when He allows it, it is only for my ultimate good—to mold me inwardly into the very image of Jesus Christ.

The peace of God carries us through the conflict. The peace of God sustains us through the tension. The peace of God lifts us in the midst of the battle.

Trust, acceptance, peace—all of these bring strength into our lives that allows us to keep hanging in there, no matter what. There is a power that begins welling up in our hearts—a power that reaches out and touches the child we love.

The Power of Committed Love

In my younger days of being a Christian, I remember much talk of power in the Christian life. Everyone wanted power. It was like some secret weapon, and if you could get it, somehow, it would sway others into acceptance of every belief you were trying to implant.

I have found that power is not so easily appropriated. Power is not a thing or a tool. It is not authority or strength. Power is simply, and profoundly, God working in and through this frail human being. Power is the quiet Spirit of God molding my life, using my life, being my life.

Power is God bringing me to maturity in Jesus Christ. The power that comes from God through my life to touch others is love.

During one of the heavy issues with our son, I wrote him a note expressing our concern for him. I told him that the love God had given us for him would be stronger than anything he might try to do to test it. I wrote that he could pull away and rebel and do his own thing, but our love would draw him back. Our love was stronger than his rebellion.

For a long time our love was severely tested. But it did win. There were many hard times. There were times when we wanted to be free of the pain of loving and caring. There were times when hope sprang vibrantly alive only to be crushed with another failure. And love bled a little.

There were times when love had to be hard and even say, “You can’t live here anymore. You refuse to live by the convictions of our home. It’s your choice. Live by our rules or leave. You are free to choose how you want to live your life, but not in our home.” Love cried until there were no tears left, only our aching, broken hearts. Love stood firm and said, “We will not pay your debts or your fines. We will not finance your rebellious choices.” Love showed anger when this child stole from the family to have his way.

Love suffered in terrible pain when this child was sentenced to jail—to live with real criminals, thieves, murderers, drug dealers, and other kids who, like our son, were so tied to booze and drugs they couldn’t get their lives together.

Love showed tenderness and affection when this child reached out in even the smallest ways to see if we were still there.

The greatest reward of all came the first time our family was together again after he had spent several months in a drug program—when he hugged each one of us tightly and said, "I love you—thank you for loving me."

After nearly six years of living on the edge of hell, God reached him through the power of love. Not *our* love. Our love had limits. We couldn't see beyond our own personal hurts and frustrations. It was God's love that reached through us to this young man who so desperately needed to know that love. It was God's love, freed to flow through us because we grasped the truth of acceptance.

Our task was to redefine love as an action, not a feeling. Love was being the best person *we* could be, so our son could become the best person he could be.

Letting Go

How does a parent let go? *Should* we let go? *Can* we let go? I know of a young woman, twenty-one years old, who was in the psychiatric ward of a hospital after her third suicide attempt. Her parents had not been to see her yet, and when asked to visit said they couldn't that night, they had an important board meeting at church.

The relative who had asked them to go was shocked. The parents' attitude was: *She has chosen her life. We have ours. What she does is of no concern to us anymore.* Had these parents "let go"? Perhaps they thought they had. But their "letting go" was, in reality, a statement of their frustration and inability to handle an impossible situation. They had, in fact, not let go; they had given up. They were trying to blot all of the unpleasantness from their conscious minds.

"Letting go" is not ridding oneself of the problem. Letting go is when you reach the point in the war against rebellion in which you, in love, force your child to take responsibility for his own life. It is active, whereas giving up is passive. Letting go is when you feel you must say, "I've done all I can. I've done all I know how to do. You are determined to have things your way, and that way isn't compatible with the lifestyle we have chosen for our home. You are free to leave and do it your way, but you can no longer live under our roof expressing disrespect and contempt for everything we believe in and stand for. We'll help you find a place to live, but you will be financially responsible for yourself. You're welcome to come home to visit any time you want. If you want to have a meal with us, please call so we'll know to expect you. If you get in trouble, we'll be there for you, but not with money. If you want to continue living here, *you* will have to change because we've changed as much as we feel we can."

Don't make the mistake of "letting go" too soon. A fifteen-year-old is not capable of living on her own. Hang on with the firmness of conviction before God that you are representatives of His authority. Maybe your eighteen-year-old is not capable of living on her own, either, especially if she is involved in the drug scene; but at some point, Mom and Dad will have to come to an agreement that they are no longer responsible, and their child needs to be set free to stand or fall on her own.

This crisis point must be handled with much prayer and with a conviction of God's timing. After your child leaves, his life may speed downhill, and there will be more guilt, remorse, and thoughts that you made the wrong decision. But keep in mind that this is precisely the kind of thing that can force your child to realize that he is not ready to be autonomous. He may be able to see for the first time that life carries with it responsibility. He may recognize and remember a few words from Mom and Dad that will finally bear fruit.

If he isn't making it, and if you have left the door open for communication, you may find him ready to talk. The important thing now is to leave "I told you so" out of the picture. He doesn't need to be reminded that parents know best. His ego will be hurting badly enough. If parents truly want to be in a position to help, the best they can do is be understanding and caring and agree that it's a hard world out there.

Of course, he may make it just fine. Sometimes parents find this harder to deal with than failure. Accept it. You may see him living a lifestyle that is against everything you believe or taught him—and apparently succeeding at keeping things together. Do not be deceived. If you have the assurance that God is dealing with that young person, believe things are going according to plan.

There is no easy way to let a teenager go. For the responsible, maturing child who has a good attitude and appears to have the ability to make good decisions, it is a little easier. But for the rebellious teenager, it is nearly impossible for Mom and Dad to have any sense of rightness *any time* about giving this child the reins to his life.

But there is a time that *is* right. For the parent who is sensitive to the Spirit of God, there will be an awareness of when that time should be. But first, do everything you can to understand, to make things right, to seek help and counsel. It may mean several years of very hard living. The hope is that this child will be saved in the end.

Responding to the Hard Things

Institute in Basic Youth Conflicts speaker Bill Gothard lists three responses we should have to the hard things that come into our lives. First, we should not try to remove the problems but allow God to use them to show us our true weaknesses. Adversity can be our greatest motivation for spiritual growth. Adversity will become destructive to us if we fail to recognize and accept the hand of God behind it. Second, we should not focus on the outward circumstances, but realize we are dealing with unseen spiritual powers. Dealing with difficulties shows us how foolish it is to put our trust anywhere but in God. There is more to this life than what we see and experience, and God alone has the power to deal with the forces of evil. Third, we should stop trying harder to live for Christ by our own efforts. We must surrender our will to Christ and ask Him to live in us and through us. We must make a commitment to do what is right and make our choices based on biblical guidelines and admonitions.

One of the beautiful things that happen as we learn to trust God in the hard places is that we get the opportunity to offer to others the same counsel and comfort we have received from God.

God wastes none of our experiences. He can take the ugliest parts of our lives and turn them into something beautiful and useful. Isaiah 61:4 speaks of rebuilding the "ancient ruins," raising up the former desolations, and renewing the "ruined cities." Joel 2:25 speaks of restoring the years the "locusts have eaten." I realize that Isaiah is speaking directly to the Israelites, but I also believe "Every Scripture is God-breathed (given by His inspiration) and profitable for instruction, for reproof and conviction of sin . . . for training in righteousness. . . . So that the man (*woman, child*) of God may be complete . . . thoroughly equipped" (2 Timothy 3:16–17, words in italics in parentheses added). Ask God for *your* scriptural strengths to stand upon. And don't let go of them.

Believe that God will work a miracle in the life of your child. But first, let Him work a miracle in you.

Something to Do

1. Immerse yourself daily in the Bible. Look for God to comfort you, challenge you, and give you direction. Read Scripture passages until God touches your heart and mind. Keep a notebook. Write as God speaks. Read, reread, and read again.

2. Pray unceasingly. Keep a list and bring it before God daily. Enlist prayer partners. Be honest with them.

3. Live your life with passion and commitment. Continue to do the things you believe God has called you to do, but evaluate them. Be certain God has placed these things on your heart and that you are not yielding to pressure or persuasion from others. Be selective. Examine your responsibilities and determine if they are important enough to take you away from the family in a time of unusual need. Seek counsel.

Prayer

Our Father, who art in heaven, hallowed be thy name. Teach me how to be the person you have planned for me to be. May my child see you, in me, and be drawn to the love that never ceases but also never compromises with wrong. Love my child through me, tenderly, compassionately, wisely. Comfort me in the darkest hours. Protect my child in the folly of his choices. Bring him home. Amen.

References

These are the books, pamphlets, articles, and websites that have influenced my thinking through the course of my life with my own teenagers, in counseling with parents and teenagers, and in the writing of this book.

ABC News. "Teen Girls Discuss Their Sex Lives." http://abcnews.go.com/Primetime/Health

About.com. "Pregnancy and Sexual Activity Statistics for Teens and College," by Jackie Burrell. http://youngadults.about.com/od/healthandsafety/qt/teenpregnancy.htm

About.com. "Warning Signs of Teenage Drug Abuse." Center for Disease Control. http://parentingteens.about.com/cs/drugsofabuse

Alexander, Chris M. "Teen Drunk Driving Statistics in the U.S.," DWI Blog, July 22, 2010. www.aboutdwi.com/blog/teen-drunk-driving-statistics-in-us/

Alibrandi, Tom. *Young Alcoholics.* Minneapolis: Comp Care Publications, 1978.

American Academy of Pediatrics. Healthy Children, Ages and Stages, "Teenage Pregnancy." Last updated: 6/17/2010. www.healthychildren.org

American Cancer Society. "Child and Teen Tobacco Use." www.cancer.org/Cancer/ChildTeenTobaccoUse. Revised: 09/28/2009.

Baker, Luther. Class notes. Human Sexuality. Central Washington University, 1981.

Barr, S. J. *A Woman's Choice.* New York: Rawson Associates, 1977.

Beardsley, Lou. *A Family Love Story: Between Parent and Teenager.* Irvine, CA: Harvest House Publishers, 1975.

Benton, John. *Do You Know Where Your Children Are?* Old Tappan, NJ: Revell, 1982.

Bloom, M. V. *Adolescent-Parental Separation.* New York: Gardner Press, Inc., 1980.

Brenton, Myron. *How to Survive Your Child's Rebellious Years.* New York: Bantam Books, 1980.

Buntman, P. H., and E. M. Saris. *How to Live With Your Teenager: A Survivor's Handbook for Parents.* New York: Ballantine Books, 1991.

Buzzle.com. "Teen Drinking and Driving Facts—Teenage Drunk Driving Statistics." www.buzzle.com/articles/teen-drinking-and-driving-facts-teenage-drunk-driving-statistics, 2010.

Campbell, Dr. Ross. *How to REALLY Love Your Child.* Wheaton, IL: SP Publications, Inc., 1977.

Campbell, Dr. Ross. *How to REALLY Love Your Teenager.* Colorado Springs: David C. Cook, 2004.

CDC (Center for Disease Control). "Alcohol and Drug Use." Modified: 6/03/2010. www.cdc.gov/HealthyYouth/alcoholdrug/index.html

CDC (Center for Disease Control). "Healthy Youth: Sexual Risk Behaviors." www.cdc.gov/HealthyYouth/sexualbehaviors/index.htm

Center for Bio-Ethical Reform. "Abortion Facts," 2008. www.abortionno.org/Resources/fastfacts.html

Century Council. "Drunk Driving Research and Statistics," from the study: New Drivers Safety Study: Insights From Teens and Parents. www.centurycouncil.org/learn-the-facts/drunk-driving-research

Chaplin, James P., and T. S. Krawiec. *Systems and Theories of Psychology.* New York: Holt, Rinehart, and Winston, Inc., 1974.

Chicago Tribune. "Can Teens and Parents Coexist on Facebook?" by Heidi Stevens. www.chicagotribune.com/features

Chilman, C. S. *Adolescent Pregnancy and Childbearing: Findings From Research.* Washington, D.C.: U.S. Dept. of Health and Human Services. NIH Publication No. 81–2077. December 1980.

Coleman, J. S. *The Adolescent Society: The Social Life of the Teenager and Its Impact on Education.* New York: Free Press, 1961.

Conger, J. J., *Adolescence and Youth: Psychological Development in a Changing World,* 4th ed. New York: Harper & Row, 1991.

Comer, James P. "Drinking in Young Adolescents." *Parents,* Vol. 55, No. 2 (February 1980).

Corey, Gerald. *Theory and Practice of Counseling and Psychotherapy,* 8th ed. Florence, KY: Cengage Learning, 2008.

Cowan, Philip. *Piaget: With Feeling.* New York: Holt, Rinehart, and Winston, 1978.

Crabb, Larry J., *Effective Biblical Counseling.* Grand Rapids: Zondervan Publishing House, 1977.

Dahl, G. L. *Why Christian Marriages Are Breaking Up.* Nashville: Thomas Nelson Publishers, 1981.

Denes, Magda. *In Necessity and Sorrow.* New York: Basic Books, 1976.

Dickens, Charles. *A Tale of Two Cities.* New York: First Signet Classic Printing. The New American Library. Penguin Books, 1960.

Dinkmeyer, Don C. *Child Development: The Emerging Self.* Englewood Cliffs, NJ: Prentice-Hall, Inc., 1965.

Dobson, James. *Dare to Discipline.* Wheaton, IL: Tyndale House, 1972.

Dobson, James. *The New Strong-Willed Child.* Wheaton, IL: Tyndale House, 2007.

Dodson, Fitzhugh. *How to Father.* New York: Signet Book. The New American Library, 1974.

Dodson, Fitzhugh. *How to Parent.* New York: Signet Book. The New American Library, 1970.

Dollar, Truman E. *Teenage Rebellion: How to Recognize It, Deal With It, Prevent It.* Old Tappan, NJ: Fleming Revell, 1981.

DriveHomeSafe.com. "How Can Parents Stop Their Teen From Speeding?" www.drivehomesafe.com/article/how_parents_can_stop_their_teen_drivers_from_speeding

DWI Blog. "Teen Drunk Driving Statistics in the U.S." Chris M. Alexander. July 22, 2010. www.aboutdwi.com/blog/teen-drunk-driving-statistics-in-us

eHow. "How to Monitor a Teen's Facebook Page," by an eHow contributor. www.ehow.com/how_2086592

Elkind, David, *A Sympathetic Understanding of the Child: Birth to Sixteen,* 3rd Edition. Boston: Allyn and Bacon, 1994.

Fadely, Jack L., and Virginia H. Hosler. *Confrontation in Adolescence.* St. Louis: The C. V. Mosby Co., 1979.

Farber, Susan. "Telltale Behavior of Twins." *Psychology Today.* Volume 15, No. 1 (January 1980), 58–80.

Focus Adolescent Services. "Teen Sexual Behavior, Issues and Concerns." Copyright 2008, Focusas.com. www.focusas.com/SexualBehavior.html

Forer, Lucille K. *The Birth Order Factor.* New York: David McKay Company, Inc., 1976.

Forer, Lucille K. *Birth Order and Life Roles.* Springfield, IL: Charles C. Thomas, 1969.

Fort, Joel. *Alcohol: Our Biggest Drug Problem.* New York: McGraw-Hill, 1973.

Fritz, J. A. *The Essence of Marriage.* Grand Rapids: Zondervan, 1969.

Gibran, Kahlil. *The Prophet.* New York: Alfred A. Knopf, 1981 edition.

Gothard, Bill. "Understanding the Winds of Adversity." Institute in Basic Youth Conflicts, 1981.

Guttmacher Institute. "U.S. Teenage Pregnancies, Births, and Abortions: National and State Trends and Trends by Race and Ethnicity" (January 2010). www.Guttmacher.org

Hardin, Garrett. *Mandatory Motherhood: The True Meaning of "Right to Life."* Boston: Beacon Press, 1974.

Havighurst, Robert J. *Developmental Tasks and Education,* 3rd ed. New York: David McKay Co., 1972.

HealthNews. "Teen Pregnancy Rate Is on the Rise," by Heather Hajek (09/01/2009). www.healthnews.com/family-health/pregnancy-childbirth-parenting

Healthy Future. "New Study: Abstinence-Only Program Delays Sex in Young Adolescent" (2010). www.healthyfuturestx.org/new-study-abstinence.html

Hendrixson, L. L. "Pregnant Children: A Socio-Educational Challenge." *Human Development,* 8th ed. Guilford, CT: Dusking Publishing, 1980.

ICADV (Indiana Coalition Against Domestic Violence). "National Teen Dating Violence Awareness and Prevention Week." www.violenceresource.org/teendatingweek.htm

Ilg, Frances L., and Louise Bates Ames. *The Gesell Institute's Child Behavior: From Birth to Ten.* New York: Harper & Row, 1955.

Jenkins, Gladys Gardner, and Helen S. Schacter. *These Are Your Children.* Glenview, IL: Scott, Foreman, and Co., 1975.

Johnson, D. W. *"Reaching Out," Interpersonal Effectiveness and Self-Actualization,* 10th ed., Englewood Cliffs, NJ: Prentice-Hall, Inc., 2008.

Kennedy, Eugene. *The Heart of Loving.* Niles, OH: Argus Communications, 1973.

Kennon Transport, LLC. "Runaway Statistics and Resources." Compiled by Michael Kennon. www.kennontransport.com/runaway.html

Kesler, Jay. *Let's Succeed With Our Teenagers: An Encouraging Look at Parent-Teen Relationships.* Elgin, IL: David C. Cook, 1973.

Kesler, Jay. *Too Big to Spank*. Glendale, CA: Regal Books, 1978.

Kids Health. "Smokeless Tobacco." Reviewed by Steven Dowshen, MD. http://kidshealth.org/teen/drug_alcohol/tobacco/smokeless.html

LaHaye, Tim. *The Family That Makes It*. Colorado Springs: Victor Books, 1971.

Lambert, B. G., B. F. Rothschild, R. Atland, and B. Green. *Adolescence: Transition From Childhood to Maturity,* 2nd ed. Monterey, CA: Brooks/Cole Publishing Co., 1978.

Marin Institute. "Alcohol and Youth Facts." www.marininstitute.org/youth/alcohol_youth.htm

Marketing Charts. "Cell Phones Key to Teens' Social Lives, 47% Can Text With Eyes Closed" (2008). www.marketingcharts.com

Mashable on Facebook. "Average Teenager Sends 3,339 Texts per Month (STATS, 2010). http://mashable.com/2010/10/14/nielsen-texting-stats

Mashable on Facebook. "Teens Experiencing Facebook Fatigue Study" (June 2010). http://mashable.com/2010/06/30

Matteson, David. *Adolescence Today: Sex Roles and the Search for Identity.* Homewood, AL: Dorsey Press, 1975.

McCandless, Boyd R. *Adolescents: Behavior and Development*. Hinsdale, IL: Dryden Press, Inc., 1970.

McGraw, Dr. Phillip C. *Relationship Rescue: A Seven-Step Strategy for Reconnecting With Your Partner.* First paperback ed. New York: Hyperion, 2000.

Mittler, Peter. *The Study of Twins.* Middlesex, England: Penguin Books, 1971.

MN Adopt. "Teen Runaways" Fact Sheet. www.mnadopt.org

Mow, A. B. *Your Teenager and You*. Grand Rapids, MI: Zondervan, 1967.

Nance, Walter E., ed. *Twin Research: Part A, Psychology and Methodology.* New York: Alan R. Liss, Inc., 1978.

National Campaign to Prevent Teen and Unplanned Pregnancy. "Teen Sexual Behavior and Contraceptive Use: Data from the Youth Risk Behavior Survey" (2009). www.TheNationalCampaign.org

National Runaway Switchboard. "Welcome to the National Runaway Switchboard." www.1800runaway.org/

NIAAA (National Institute on Alcohol Abuse and Alcoholism). "Alcohol Alert." http://pubs.niaaa.nih.gov/publications/aa67/aa67.htm. Number 67 (January 2008).

NIDA (National Institute on Drug Abuse). "High School and Youth Trends." www.drugabuse.gov/infofacts/HSYouthtrends.html

NIDA (National Institute on Drug Abuse). "InfoFacts: Marijuana." www.nida.nih.gov/infofacts/marijuana.html Data from the 2009 Monitoring the Future Survey, funded by the NIDA, NIH, DHHS.

NIDA (National Institute on Drug Abuse). "Marijuana: Facts for Teens." Revised March 2008. www.nida.nih.gov/marijbroch/Marijteens.html

Nielsenwire. "U.S. Teen Mobile Report: Calling Yesterday, Texting Today, Using Apps Tomorrow" (2010). http://blog.nielsen.com

Online Safety Site. "Teen Internet Statistics" (2010). www.onlinesafetysite.com/P1/Teenstats.htm

Osborne, Cecil G. *The Art of Understanding Your Mate*. Grand Rapids, MI: Zondervan, 1970.

Oxford Dictionary of Phrase, Saying, and Quotation, 2nd ed. Edited by Susan Ratcliffe. New York: Oxford University Press, 2002.

Pace, R. W., B. D. Peterson, and M. D. Burnett. *Techniques for Effective Communication*. Reading, PA: Addison-Wesley Publishing Co., 1979.

Powell, John. *The Secret of Staying in Love*. Allen, TX: Thomas More Associates, 1995.

Rice, F. Philip. *The Adolescent: Development, Relationships, and Culture*, 11th ed. Boston: Allyn and Bacon, Inc., 2005.

Rocky Mountain Insurance Information Association. "Teen Driving Statistics" (2010). www.rmiia.org/auto/teens/Teen_Driving_Statistics.asp

Runaway Teens.org. "Overall Runaway Statistics." www.runawayteens.org/statistics.html

Safe Teen Driving. "FAQ about Teen Driver Safety" (2010). www.safeteen-driving.org/faq/faq.php

Schaefer, Earl S. *Parental Attitudes and Child Behavior.* Springfield, IL: Charles C. Thomas Publisher, 1961.

Schowalter, John E., and Walter R. Anyan. *The Family Handbook of Adolescence*. New York: Alfred A. Knopf, 1981.

SearchTime.Com. "Parents' Sex Talk With Kids: Too Little, Too Late," by Alice Park (December 07, 2009). www.time.com/time/health/article

Sebald, Hans. *Adolescence: A Social Psychological Analysis,* 4th ed. Englewood Cliffs, NJ: Prentice-Hall, Inc. 1992.

Shedd, Charlie. *You Can Be a Great Parent*. Nashville: W Publishing Group, 1982.

Teen Chat Decoder. "Teens and Sexting" (February 16, 2010). www.teenchat-decoder.com/607/teens-and-sexting/

Teen Help. "Teen Alcohol Abuse Statistics" (2010). www.teenhelp.com/teen-alcohol-use/teen-alcohol-abuse-statistics.html

Tessler, Diane. J. *Drugs, Kids, and Schools*. Santa Monica, CA: Goodyear Publishing Co., 1980.

Thompson, C. L., and W. A. Poppen. *For Those Who Care: Ways of Relating to Youth*. Columbus, OH: Charles E. Merrill, 1972.

Toman, Walter. *Family Constellation: Its Effect on Personality and Social Behavior,* 3rd ed. New York: Springer Publishing, 1976.

Trobisch, Walter. *Love Yourself.* Downers Grove, IL: InterVarsity Press, 1976.

U.S. Department of Health and Human Services. "Teenagers in the United States: Sexual Activity, Contraceptive Use, and Childbearing." National Survey of Family Growth (2006–2008). Hyattsville, MD: DHHS Publication (PHS), 2010.

Wahlroos, Sven. Family Communication: A Guide to Emotional Health. New York: Plume, 1983.

Wakefield, Norman. *Listening: A Christian's Guide to Loving Relationships.* Waco, TX: Word Books, 1981.

Weaver, Richard L. *Understanding Interpersonal Communication,* 5th ed. Glenville, IL: Scott, Foresman, 1990.

White, John. *Parents in Pain: Overcoming the Hurt and Frustration of Problem Children*. Downers Grove, IL: InterVarsity Press, 1979.

Williams, Roger J. *You Are Extraordinary.* New York: Pyramid Publications, 1976.

Wright, H. Norman. *Communication: Key to Your Marriage.* Ventura, CA: Regal Books, 2000.

CONNIE RAE, LMHC is a licensed mental health counselor. She received her Bachelor's degree in Psychology from Seattle Pacific University, and her Master's degree in Family Studies at Central Washington University. Connie has worked with individuals and families with youth at risk for more than twenty-five years. She has been a speaker at conferences, seminars, and workshops, and has taught classes in family issues. She and her husband, Dennis, have raised four children, and adopted a fifth as a teenager. They have seventeen grandchildren. Dennis is a retired junior high and middle school teacher. Connie is in semi-retirement and enjoying the process of sharing her experiences through her writing. They live in Wenatchee, Washington.

Connie Rae welcomes any questions, comments, or responses to what you have read in this book. You may contact her through her website: helpandhopeforyou.com